# St. John On Foot And By Car

D0816262

A Walking And Motor Guide
To the History and Natural Beauty of
St. John, U.S. Virgin Islands

Revised Edition

## By Randall S. and Rebecca S. Koladis

**Photography By Joshua S. Koladis**

Copyright 2001 By Randall S. and Rebecca S. Koladis
Library of Congress Control Number: 2001131380
ISBN 0-9708919-0-3

*Layout and Design:*
Joshua Seaward Koladis

*Editorial Assistance:*
Rachel Star Koladis
Sarah Rose Koladis

*Published By:*
## ISLAND WAYS
P.O. Box 270031
West Hartford, Connecticut 06127

# Contents

*Cruz Bay Harbor*

# St. John and the Book

## St. John and the U.S. Virgin Islands

There are three major islands in the U.S. Virgin Islands archipelago, which includes 68 islands in total and measures 133 square miles. The largest islands are St. Croix, followed by St. Thomas, then tiny St. John - the latter totaling only 21 square miles. Of the three major islands, St. John is by far the most virgin! The untouched natural beauty of this tropical paradise is due primarily to the creation of the Virgin Islands National Park, which today encompasses nearly three-fifths of the island.

Although many thousands of people visit St. John each year, the island has only about 3,000 inhabitants. There are no shopping malls on St. John, no high-rise resorts, no casinos and no traffic lights. This is a quiet island where life moves at half-speed. St. John is a great place to simply relax and unwind.

St. John does not have an airstrip. Most visitors arrive in Cruz Bay, the principal port of entry, by cruise ship or ferry boat, which takes less than 20 minutes to get here from neighboring St. Thomas. Stepping onto the dock, one becomes immediately entranced by the picturesque setting of the village.

# VI National Park

The Virgin Islands National Park was made possible through the generosity of Mr. Laurence S. Rockefeller and members of his family. Mr. Rockefeller first discovered the beauty of the island when he came here on a sailing vacation some fifty years ago.

In November 1954, the Rockefeller family began acquiring large tracts of land. The plan was to eventually turn the acreage over to the federal government for the establishment of a national park. The Rockefellers initially accumulated over 5,000 acres of land, which they donated to the Department of the Interior. On August 2, 1956, President Eisenhower signed a bill authorizing the creation of the Virgin Islands National Park. Over the years, the size of the park has grown steadily. Today it totals more than 9,620 acres plus an additional 5,600 acres of off-shore underwater marine gardens.

Mr. Rockefeller's visionary gesture spared St. John from overdevelopment. Instead, St. John has remained an unspoiled jewel whose captivating beauty offers unending pleasure and enjoyment to everyone who comes here.

St. John
Virgin Islands National Park

In the 1950s, Cruz Bay replaced Coral Bay (a smaller settlement on the east side of the island) as St. John's main center of commerce. Commercial businesses in the village consist primarily of several well-stocked grocery stores, one bank, a post office, dive centers, a couple of gas stations and a few dozen duty-free shops.

## Getting Around

St. John is an easy island to explore. It measures only 9 miles long by 3 miles wide. Jeeps and other 4-wheel drive vehicles are a popular and fun way to get around. Visitors can ferry cars over from St. Thomas, but most choose to rent vehicles at one of several car rental agencies in Cruz Bay

Taxis are readily available for hire. Colorful group taxis called "safari" buses are a popular means of transportation. You will find them lined up and waiting for passengers at the entrance to the ferry dock. Taxi drivers are friendly and courteous. Most are well informed about the history and culture of their island and make excellent tour guides. For years, Miss Lucy has been one of St. John's most colorful taxi drivers. Her trademark is a set of flower-bedecked cow horns, which she likes to keep mounted on the front hood of her "cab."

There is also public bus service (operated by Vitran). Buses run regularly between the ferry dock in Cruz Bay and Salt Pond Beach, located on the south end of the island. Unfortunately, the bus route will not take you to any of the popular North Side beaches like Trunk Bay.

The village communications center called Connections is a good place to stop and get orientated. It is located up Prindsen Gade (Danish for "Prince Street") just a few steps from the ferry dock. Connections provides free literature about things to see and do on St. John. They also offer visitors public telephones and fax machines.

*Administration Bldg*

The National Park Service Visitor Center is where you should go to pick up trail maps and information about national park activities and programs. The Visitor Center is located opposite the entrance to Mongoose Junction *(See Cruz Bay map, pg. 24)*.

While staying on St. John, you may decide to take a day trip to one of the nearby British Virgin Islands such as Tortola or Virgin Gorda. If so, you would depart from The Customs House, which operates out of a little white building located adjacent to the parking lot just in front of the Administration Building. The Administration Building is the imposing white structure situated atop the little peninsula overlooking the harbor.

A great spot to check out local happenings is the community message board. It is prominently displayed at the street corner just beyond Connections (diagonally across the street from the bank). Here you will find announcements for fish fries, meetings, reggae concerts and other local events.

## The Book and How It Works

*St. John On Foot and By Car* is designed to give visitors an opportunity to experience personally the history

*Messsage Board*

and natural beauty of St. John. It features a collection of 4 self-guided tours, which can be followed in any order. Tours can be combined with a lunch, some shopping or a swim.

# St. John Attractions

### Sun & Fun

St. John's talcum-white beaches and dazzling-clear waters are world-renowned for swimming and sun-bathing. Just a few feet off-shore scuba divers and snorkelers enjoy the pleasure of exploring miles of coral reefs teeming with colorful sea life. Other popular visitor activities include kayaking, hiking, fishing, sailing, sunbathing, horseback riding and ecological tours.

### Fauna and Flora

Moving inland, vacationers discover another treasure - the wealth of the forest, with its abundantly rich array of fauna and flora. Hikers can penetrate the dense greenery of St. John with relative ease, thanks to an elaborate network of well-cleared paths. Bicycling is not a popular activity on St. John due to the steep hills and narrow, winding roads.

## Diversity of People

Many different cultures come together here, including African, English, Danish, Dutch, Spanish and U.S. These diverse cultural backgrounds are reflected in the food, speech, habits and artistic expression of the islanders.

## Historic Sites

The architecture of many of St. John's buildings reflect the colonial Danish influence. The habit of driving on the left is also a Danish remnant. Old plantation names such as Carolina, Enighed and Adrian are used to identify various areas of the island.

For a first-hand sense of the past, you will want to tour an old Danish sugar plantation. The best-preserved ruins are at Annaberg, Cinnamon Bay and Reef Bay. The ghost-like images of these abandoned structures are haunting reminders of the history of slavery on St. John.

## Indian Artifacts

Artifacts of pre-Columbian Indians have been discovered on St. John. Most notable are the Taino Indian "petroglyphs" ( rock carvings) found along the Reef Bay Trail. Many Taino pottery images have been unearthed at Cinnamon Bay.

*Zemi Deity, By C.E. Taylor*

At the back of the book helpful factual information can be found as well as recommendations on sources for obtaining additional aid in planning your trip to St. John. ***The 4 tours are arranged as follows:***

## WALKING TOUR OF CRUZ BAY (2.5 HOURS)

This tour begins with a visit to the National Park Visitor

Center followed by a short hike out to the Lind Battery. Here visitors enjoy a scenic view of Cruz Bay harbor. The trail passes through open dry forest where visitors are exposed to a variety of cactuses and arid vegetation.

Returning to the village, the route skirts the harbor and brings you to the Administration Building (a former 18th-century fortress) after which come stops at the Ivan Jadan Museum and the Elaine Ione Sprauve Library & Museum. This is a pleasurable and informative way to combine a tour of the village with some casual shopping and a lunch.

## MOTOR TOUR OF THE NORTH SIDE (4.5 HOURS)

Exploring the North Side, visitors will have a chance to experience stunning beaches like Trunk Bay and Hawksnest. A highlight of the tour is a visit to the popular sugar plantation ruins at Annaberg. The stop at Cinnamon Bay has several interesting facets, including a brief history/nature hike, which winds past a sugar factory and an old Danish cemetery plot. The path is shaded and there are plaques identifying tropical vegetation along the way. Cinnamon is

*Archeological Dig*

also where a recent archeological dig has uncovered many ancient pre-Columbian artifacts made by the Taino Indians. This tour is highly recommended for first-time visitors.

## MOTOR TOUR OF CENTERLINE ROAD AND THE EAST AND SOUTH SIDES (4.5 HOURS)

Stops on this tour include the Cathrineberg ruins, Emmaus Moravian Church and spectacular mountaintop views of Coral Bay and the BVI. Coral Bay is the site of the original Danish settlement on St. John as well as the site of the historic slave revolt of 1733-34. The tour includes a visit to the unique East End community whose residents have long been known for their skills as carpenters, stone masons, boat builders and basket makers. It concludes with stops at popular Salt Pond Beach and Lameshur Bay. These are both excellent swimming

*Salt Pond, Salt Pond Beach*

beaches. At Lameshur visitors can tour the ruins of a 19th-century bay rum still. You will also have the opportunity to see where astronauts conducted pioneering underwater experiments over 30 years ago as part of the U.S. space program's important Tektite mission.

### HIKE DOWN THE REEF BAY TRAIL (5 HOURS, ROUND TRIP)

A full-day hike into St. John's fascinating world of fauna and flora. Hikers visit ancient Indian rock carvings made by pre-Columbian Indians and tour the abandoned ruins of the last operating sugar processing plant on St. John. Much of the steam-powered machinery is still in place. The trail is 2.2 miles in length and descends a mountainside through dense moist and dry tropical forests

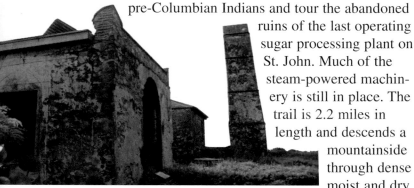

*Reef Bay Sugar Factory*

filled with exotic vegetation, much of which is identified by informative national park plaques. The beach at Reef Bay makes an ideal spot for a picnic and swim.

## Useful Tips

Before getting started, you will want to be mindful of a few local customs:

(1)     Remember to drive on the left. Avoid traffic tickets by making certain that the driver and front seat passengers wear

seat belts at all times. Children must use child seats if they are less than 5 years old or weigh less than 40 pounds. Fines are stiff! $100 for either infraction. Illegally parking in a handicap space can cost you $1000! When renting a vehicle, be aware of any restrictions. Car rental agencies have specified certain roads as off-limits because of rough conditions. Be extra careful when it is raining. The switchbacks can get very slippery when wet.

(2)     Islanders are in the habit of greeting each other with a friendly "Good Morning" or "Good Evening" when passing one another or before commencing conversation. Try it!

**Whoops!**

(3)     The sun shines very intensely here. When at the beach, try not to overdo it! Wear sun block. Also, when swimming, beware of heavy surf. It can get especially rough on the North Side beaches during the winter months.

(4)     St. Johnians are very modest people. Women are not permitted to wear bathing suits in town, and men should wear shirts.

(5)     Remember to keep valuables protected, particularly when swimming at the beach. Petty crime exists, even in paradise.

CAUTION
DO NOT LEAVE VALUABLES
UNATTENDED

$1,000 FINE FOR DUMPING ON GROUND FREE DUMP AT CENTER-LINE AND GIFFT HILL

# National Park Rules and Regulations

As you will likely be spending a great deal of your vacation time within the boundaries of the national park, it would be helpful to be aware of a few of the more basic park rules and regulations:

**(1)**    Collecting plants and animals (dead or alive) or inanimate objects including cultural artifacts is prohibited. Metal detectors are not allowed anywhere in the park. However, the gathering by hand for personal use or consumption of the following is permitted: coconuts, genips, limes, mammy apples, soursops, hog plums, papaya, mangoes, guavas, sweet limes, sugar apples, seagrapes and all seeds.

*Petroglyph*

**(2)**    Fishing is allowed outside of swim areas, but not in Trunk or Jumbie Bays. Spearguns are prohibited anywhere in or on park waters.

**(3)**    Camping is allowed only at Cinnamon Bay Campground.

**(4)**    Waterskiing/jetskiing is not permitted in park waters.

**(5)**    Kayaks, dinghies, rafts or any other motored or rowed vessels must stay in marked dinghy channels and outside swim areas.

**(6)**    Fires are permitted only in grills at designated picnic areas.

**(7)**    Feeding of marine and terrestrial wildlife is prohibited.

*Beach Treasure*

**(8)**    Pets must be leashed and are prohibited from all park beaches.

**(9)**    Glass bottles are not permitted on park beaches and public places.

**(10)**    Coral is easily damaged by anchors and human touch. Please refrain from touching!

* You are asked not to climb on any of the ruins, as this can cause damage and may result in personal injury.

St. John belongs to the archipelago commonly referred to as the Virgin Islands (which includes both the U.S. and British Virgins). The group lies 1100 miles southeast of Miami and 1600 miles south of New York. Like most other islands in the Antilles chain, the Virgin Islands are quite hilly, being of volcanic origin.

Christopher Columbus accidentally discovered the Virgin Islands in 1493 on his second voyage to the New World. So numerous and so beautiful were the islands, that Columbus was reminded of the fabled beauty of Saint Ursula and her renowned army of virgins who were massacred by the Huns during the Middle Ages. He named the group "Santa Ursula y Las Once Mil Virgenes" in their memory.

Although Columbus maneuvered his fleet to within a few miles of St. John's coast, he did not come ashore. He probably feared the island might be inhabited by fierce Carib Indians. He had recently skirmished with some Caribs on nearby St. Croix. Actually, had he braved a landing he would have discovered that it was Taino Indians, not Caribs, who were living on St. John at the time of his arrival.

*Male Indian*
*By C.E. Taylor*

Tainos were a nation of peaceful Indians who proliferated the eastern Caribbean until the early 1500s, when they even-

tually became extinct through contact with western civiliza-
tion. The small
number that lived on
St. John supported
themselves by fish-
ing, gathering food
from the land and
by growing produce.

*Indian Canoe*

A hundred years after Columbus' visit, Sir Francis Drake,
like his predecessor also passed close by St. John without
landing. Drake was en-route to his history-making attack on
the Spanish stronghold on Puerto Rico.

Another one hundred years slipped lazily by, and nobody
seemed to pay any further attention to tiny St. John. Then,
towards the end of the 17th century, squatters began arriving
from the Danish island of St. Thomas and the nearby British
possession of Tortola. As their numbers grew, friction developed between the two nationalities. From time-to-time, spo-
radic fighting broke out. At first, neither the English nor
Danish home governments cared enough about St. John to
assert a formal claim to the island.

Finally in 1717, acting on a charter granted by King
Christian V, the Danish West India and Guinea Company
made the first official move to settle St. John. Estate Caroline
(the company plantation) was staked out in Coral Bay, and a
fort was constructed on the north side of the harbor.

This upset the English settlers. Some complaints were
lodged. At one point, a gunboat was even dispatched from
Tortola to scare off the Danish "intruders." No shots were
fired, however. Instead, the warship turned around half-way to
St. John, and sailed back to Tortola. No further resistance was
offered. Thus the Danes took control of the island and turned

to the task of stabilizing their new possession. In order to attract settlers, the home government offered generous tax breaks to persons who would clear the land for cultivation of sugar, cotton and tobacco. The incentives worked. Plantations were developed, and the island soon became fairly prosperous.

*Early Plantation Scene, Artist Unknown*

But early prosperity was tenuous. It was dependent upon the importation of slaves, who were being brought to St. John from the west coast of Africa by way of St. Thomas. Slave trafficking was a key part of the infamous Triangle Trade. This unholy enterprise took its name from its triangular pattern, which worked as follows: European merchants, eager to barter goods manufactured in their own countries, would bring their products to the west coast of Africa where they were exchanged for slaves. The slaves were then transported to the West Indies, where they were traded for cotton, sugar and tobacco, which was then hauled back to Europe and exchanged for manufactured goods.

In 1733, the slave trade was nearly at its peak, when St. John suffered a devastating slave revolt. At the time, St. John had 109 plantations in existence. The island population was 208 whites and 1414 blacks, most of whom were slaves.

Almost half of the plantations were destroyed in the revolt, which lasted six long months. After the revolt a few

# Slave Revolt

In 1733, optimism was running high on St. John. To many, there seemed no limit to how big tiny St. John might grow. But then, in the early morning hours of Sunday, November 23, disaster struck in the form of a fierce slave revolt, which gripped the island in a horrific nightmare of terror and havoc.

Nothing seemed out of the ordinary on the fateful morning to the lone sentry on duty at the fort in Coral Bay as he watched a small group of slaves slowly making it's way up the hillside

*Freedom Statue*

toward the fort. "Ah, slaves with wood," he thought as the group drew near. The guard knew it was customary for slaves to bring wood to the fort every Sunday. Sensing nothing unusual, he jumped down from his watchtower and opened the gates.

*Coral Bay Relic*

Once inside, the slaves produced cane knives, which had been carefully hidden in their bundles of wood. They pounced on the unsuspecting guard, and quickly hacked him to death. There were seven other soldiers asleep in the guardhouse at the time. They might have been slightly aroused by the scuffle outside, but before they could fully awaken, the rebels had battered down the door, and swarmed down on the defenseless men. Within minutes, the mutilated bodies of six of the seven soldiers lay dead on the floor. One soldier managed to escape and make his way over to St. Thomas, where he spread the alarm.

Leaving the guardhouse, the rebels mounted the gun-deck and fired two blasts on a cannon, which signaled the start of the revolt. With the aid of drums and horns made of conch shells, word of the revolt spread quickly around the island. Slaves marched from one plantation to the next, ransacking great houses, setting fire to cane fields, and murdering white masters and overseers.

In Coral Bay at Estate Caroline, Judge Sodtmann, the son-in-law of Governor Gardelin, was singled out and brutally butchered before the terror-stricken eyes of his twelve-year-old daughter, who was later murdered as well. The rebels hated the judge because of the harsh sentences he had imposed upon island slaves. As punishment, they made the judge dance in a circle on a table (mimicking the manner in which slaves were often forced to dance for the entertainment of the masters) while they sliced at his legs with their cane knives. The judge eventually slipped in his own blood and fell to the ground whereupon the slaves stabbed him through the heart.

*Courtesy "Vore Gamie Tropekolonier"*

Over at Caneel Bay, about forty planters gathered at the home of Peter Durloe. With the aid of a small cannon, they were able to hold off the rebels just long enough to escape in a boat that arrived from St. Thomas.

The Danes were unable to restore order. "We pursued the blacks over the mountain all the way to Coral Bay," wrote Governor Gardelin to the Danish king shortly after the start of the revolt. "Arriving below the fort we attacked a band of rebels in force on the hill. After a sharp engagement in which we lost two men, we succeeded in recapturing the fort. During the charge several blacks were captured. Our forces being insufficient to garrison the fort, we abandoned it after spiking the guns. The next day we captured twenty men and women besides three who attempted to escape to Tortola in a boat. We beheaded ten, but they were only followers, not leaders. I am fearful," Gardelin concluded, "that it will take a long time before we catch the instigators of this bloody insurrection."

Several unsuccessful attempts were made at crushing the rebellion, including two tries with the help of English troops from Tortola. Finally, in May 1734, the Danes were able to regain control of the island, but it required the assistance of two French warships and a full company of soldiers dispatched from Martinique.

When the end was near, many of the rebel slaves deliberately jumped to their deaths from the cliffs at Mary Point. Others committed suicide at Brown Bay.

*Caneel Ruins*

settlers returned to St. John, but many chose instead to get a "fresh start" on the yet undeveloped island of St. Croix. In time, a few plantations were rebuilt, and, for a short while anyway, St. John seemed to regain some of its former prosperity.

But renewed stability did not last long. Back home, Denmark became involved in the Napoleonic Wars and took sides with France against England. British troops from Tortola took advantage of the situation and twice attacked and captured St. John; once briefly in 1801 and again in 1807. The second occupation lasted seven years and had a numbing effect on the St. John economy. Two other 19th-century developments, the perfection of the sugar beet and the emancipation of the slaves in 1848, nearly brought an end to the plantation system.

St. John's economy staged another brief recovery towards the end of the 19th century when a new strain of sugar cane was imported from Java. The Java cane required less care to cultivate and would supposedly

*Cultivating Cane*
*Courtesy New York Public Library*

yield more sugar per stalk. To process the new cane, modern steam-powered equipment was installed at several of St. John's remaining plantations.

Unfortunately, the new cane failed to generate sufficient

*Steam Powered Machinery, Reef Bay*

profits, and one-by-one, St. John's sugar plantations ceased operations for good. The last operating plantation at Reef Bay was shut down in 1916.

With the collapse of the sugar economy, nobody paid much attention to the island. The few natives who remained on St. John supported themselves by fishing, raising livestock and growing small vegetable gardens. Not even the purchase of the Virgin Islands by the United States in 1917 caused much commotion. The U.S. purchased the islands for $24 million as a defense against alleged intentions by the German government to use them as U-boat bases.

At first the U.S. government paid little attention to the Virgin Islands. Indeed, residents were not even given citizenship until 1927. But then, following the end of WWII, tourism suddenly blossomed in the Caribbean, and everything changed. With the creation of the Virgin Islands National Park in 1954, St. John suddenly awoke. Visitors began arriving in ever-increasing numbers. Today St. John has become one of the most popular tourist destinations in the world.

# A Walking Tour of Cruz Bay

The village of Cruz Bay, affectionately referred to locally as Love City, is the principal settlement on St. John. Here visitors will find gift shops and many fine restaurants. Most of the shops are concentrated in Wharfside Village and at Mongoose Junction. Wharfside Village is a brightly colored collection of small stores located immediately to the right of the ferry landing. Mongoose Junction, a peaceful cluster of charming stone buildings and courtyards filled with quaint boutiques, is located near the

*Morgan's Mango*

National Park Visitor Center. The shops at both locations are filled with fine jewelry, ceramics, clothing, local artwork and unusual gift items, some of which are produced on the premises by local craftsmen. Cruz Bay is also where most of St. John's "nightlife" takes place.

*Mongoose Junction*

As a convenience, visitors will find public restrooms locat-

ed directly behind Mongoose Junction and at the end of the parking lot immediately adjacent to the entrance to the St. John Administration Building.

You begin your walking tour of Cruz Bay at the National

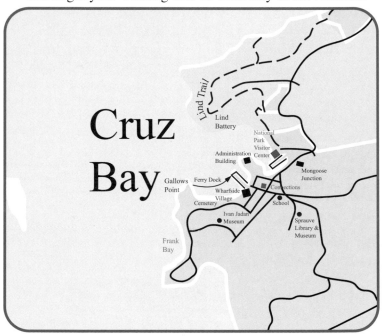

Park Visitor Center located on the left side of the harbor.

## National Park Visitor Center

The National Park Visitor Center is a 5-minute walk from the ferry. The Visitor Center was established to provide tourists with useful information about the recreational facilities of the Virgin Islands National Park. In addition to natural history books and a selection of gift items for sale in their retail shop, the center offers literature on park programs, wildlife and historic sites on the island.

Assisting the National Park Service efforts is a local, non-profit group known as the Friends of the National Park. The Friends sponsor a variety of cultural and educational classes

*Visitor Center*

that are open to the public. Ask for a copy of their brochure at the Visitor Center.

Rangers working at the center are more than happy to answer questions. They can give you information about the Park Service's interpretive programs. The programs typically feature events such as a hike down the Reef Bay Trail, bird-watching at Francis Bay, a ranger guided tour through the ruins at Cinnamon Bay or Annaberg or a snorkeling tour along the Trunk Bay underwater trail.

The Visitor Center is open daily, 8:00 a.m. to 4:30 p.m. Tel: (340) 776-6201.

# Friends of the National Park

The Friends of the National Park is a non-profit, island organization working with the National Park Service to help protect and conserve our Virgin Islands National Park. The Friends objective is to help safeguard the resources of the park while enhancing the experience of visitors. The Friends publishes a brochure of classes and trips, which can be obtained at the National Park Visitor Center. Typical classes open to the public include palm weaving, coastal ecology, island marine biology, the history of scientific research on St. John, West Indian cooking, and archeology of St. John. For additional information call (340) 779-4940 or you may e-mail Friends at friends@islands.vi. Information can also be found on the Friends' internet site at www.friendsvinp.org.

*Scientific Reserach Center*

To continue on, find your way to the beginning of the Lind Battery Trail. The entrance is located directly behind the National Park Visitor Center. It takes only 10 minutes to hike out to the site of the former British gun battery overlooking the harbor. The original gun emplacements are gone, but the view of Cruz Bay harbor from the overlook where the battery was once located is quite nice. You might want to bring along a small bottle of water. This is an uphill climb, passing through arid, scrub vegetation. It can get quite hot as the day wears on. The distance to the overlook is approximately 0.4 miles.

## Lind Battery

A gun battery was constructed at Lind Point by the English during one of their two occupations; either 1801 or 1807 (nobody seems quite sure as to the correct date). According to local legend, the fortification was erected in a single night by a detachment of British troops, which landed secretly along the seaward side of the hill. The men worked feverously throughout the night, hauling heavy weapons up the steep slope. When the residents of Cruz Bay awoke the next morning, they were startled and intimidated by the British guns. They quickly surrendered without a fight.

This is a good spot to start familiarizing yourself with

local vegetation. Coconut palms can be easily spotted along the waterfront below. During the summer months of July and August you will also be able to pick out the brilliant orange-red blossoms of the graceful flamboyant tree. The flamboyant was carried to St. John from Madagascar.

When you are ready to depart, retrace your steps back down the trail. Go past the National Park Visitor Center and turn right at the end of the drive onto North Shore Road in front of Mongoose Junction. After passing St. John Car Rental, turn right onto Droningens Gade, which takes you to the entrance gate leading up to the Administration Building.

## Administration Building

In 1734, a fortress known as "Christian fort of St. Jan" was constructed on this site. It was only one year after the slave revolt. The purpose of the fort was to protect

the island's white residents from future uprisings. Unlike most seacoast fortifications, its guns trained inland on its own population! Besides a battery, the fortress also contained a courthouse, torture chambers, dungeon and a whipping post. Today the building houses various government offices.

The bars on the window of the original dungeon (located in the building left of the driveway) are still visible. There is an ancient plaque on the wall bearing a glowing epitaph to the building's creator. It reads: "Constructed by Freedman James Wright, born on St. John who thereafter earned his freedom with the enterprise and good behavior

which gained his superiors favor and his fellow citizens respect among whom he holds the position of first lieutenant in the Brigade on St. Thomas 1825."

Our next stop is the Ivan Jadan Museum. The museum is located on Lavender Hill just beyond Gallows Point. It is about a 10-minute walk from the Administration Building. The museum is best reached by turning right at the end of the driveway of the Administration Building and proceeding down Droningens Gade past the ferry dock.

The park opposite the ferry dock is a good place to rest and perhaps sample some local cooking, which is often on sale here. The statute in the park comemorating the freedom of the slaves is worth noting. There is also an interesting metal sculpture of the mocko jumbie, or West Indian "ghost," positioned in front of the Cruz Bay Beach Shop.

Continuing on, proceed down Strand Gade at the Cruz Bay Beach Shops. Going past the Catholic Church, turn right again and follow the road along the harbor's edge towards Gallows Point. This area is called "Gallows Point" because it is the spot where convicted slaves were publicly tortured and frequently executed.

Conch shells were often placed on island graves to ward off evil spirits. Notice the decorated cemetery plots on either side of the road.

Just past Gallows Point Resort is Genip Street on the left. The entrance to the Ivan Jadan museum is located up this street near the top of the hill. If you were to continue down the road instead of turning to go up Genip Street, you would come to Frank Bay, a favorite swimming beach for in-town residents. Ask about the octopus at Frank Bay when you get to the museum

# Island Foods

Local West Indian dishes are a mixture of African and European heritage with a large dousing of good old fashion imagination thrown in. Some local dishes were passed

down from plantation days when slaves were required to obtain their food from gardens they cultivated in what little free time they had. Extra produce was sold on Sundays to generate income. Following Emancipation, the few hundred persons who continued to live here learned to survive by "getting by" with what was available locally. Sweet potatoes, yams, pumpkins (yellow squash), peas, fish, turtles, whelks, conchs and livestock formed the basic ingredients of their diet.

Traditional native foods are Johnnycakes (fried bread), fungi (a corn meal preparation), pate (a dumpling filled with spicy meat or fish), kallaloo (a spicy combination of boiled fish and local greens), fish chowder, fried fish fillets and chicken with rice. Popular desserts are coconut sugar cakes, sliced mangoes and soursop ice cream.

# Ivan Jadan Museum

The Ivan Jadan Museum houses over 5,000 letters, documents, artifacts and photos related to the life and singing career of Ivan Jadan, a Soviet dissident and one of the great Russian tenors of the 20th century. Having escaped from Stalin's Russia, Jadan eventually found freedom on St. John. Here he spent 40 years living and enjoying his island paradise along with his wife, Doris, the museum's curator. Doris is more than happy to talk to visitors about Ivan's incredible life and his many adventures. She herself is the author of several books including *A Guide to the Natural History of St. John* and *Virgin Island Cuisine with Ivan and Christine* as well as her latest book entitled *Ivan Jadan*.

When you are ready to depart the museum, retrace your steps back toward the ferry dock. Reaching the Cruz Bay Beach Shop, turn right and proceed up Prindsen Gade passing the Lutheran Church on your right.

Continue up the road past the bank and the police

# Carnival

Carnival is part of a 30-day occurance commencing in early June and culminating with the July 4th celebration of Cultural Day. The event features bike races, calypso shows, parades and fireworks. The celebration period encompasses Organic Act Day (third Monday in June), Carnival and Emancipation Day (July 3rd). The latter commemorates the Danes freeing of the slaves in 1848.

Carnival has its origins in plantation times, although St. John did not officially celebrate its first carnival until 1928. Originally carnival was devised as a form of entertainment to make the slaves happier and motivate them to work harder. It typically coincided with the Christian Easter and Christmas celebrations. As a part of the festivities, slaves donned costumes and mimicked their masters through song and dance.

The traditional figure associated with carnival is the mocko jumbie, a shape-changing ghost-like figure, whose origins are traced to West Africa. The jumbie appears at night and is known for terrifying those who have misbehaved. At carnival, the jumbie appears on stilts dressed in elaborate pants and jacket made of colorful silks and satins.

# Island Patois

Newcomers are often confused by native islander's use of language and words. Eva Boulon, talks with humor about the peculiarity of the local "language" in her entertaining book, *My Island Kitchen*. "I have always had trouble understanding the natives odd usage of words" she writes reflecting on her early days on St. John "as well as the unexpected rhythmic, almost singing quality to their speech. For instance, while we were still camping on the beach, our house boy, George, who was slightly scornful of this informal way of living, confronted me one fine afternoon when I came dripping out of the sea from a lovely swim and said, 'Madam, shall I catch the fire?' I had visions of George," recalls Ms. Boulon, "darting after a fleeing flame until I realized he was asking about lighting the fire!"

*Author's Note: Unfortunately Ms. Boulon's book is no longer in print, but it is available for reading at the Elaine Ione Sprauve Library in Cruz Bay.*

station. The road forks at the Texaco Gas Station. Bear right. A short distance beyond the gas station, take your first right at the Anglican Church. A few yards ahead on the left, you arrive at the last stop on the tour, The Elaine Ione Sprauve Library & Museum.

# Elaine Ione Sprauve Library & Museum

The Elaine Ione Sprauve Library & Museum is housed in what was previously called the Enighed Estate House, one of the

first non-wooden structures to be built on St. John. The original estate house was destroyed by fire earlier in the century and has just recently been restored. The Enighed House is listed on the National Register of Historic Places. For those interested in Caribbean history, the library has an extensive collection of reference books. The library is open Monday-Friday, 9 am to 5 pm.

In the basement of the library you will find the museum. It contains an eclectic assortment of artifacts, curious old photos and documents, as well as replicas of buildings found on the

island. Items recovered from the wreck of the HMS Santa
Monica, examples of hoop basket
making and a photo of a
Bordeaux Mt. daub and wattle
house (woven sticks and mud) are
among the fascinating items on
display here. This is a great place
to spend some  time when you
are having an overcast or rainy
day!

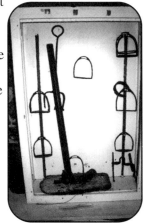

*This concludes the walking tour of Cruz Bay.*

## Getting Started

The North Side tour begins at the historic Caneel Bay Plantation resort. It is located along North Shore Road a little less than a mile from Cruz Bay. *(See centerfold map, pgs. 74-75, for North Shore tour route.)* Certain areas of the resort are restricted to hotel guests, but many amenities, including most of the restaurants, the gift shop and beach are open to the general public. There is a security guard at the entrance to the drive leading into the resort. Let the guard know your destination. He will direct you to the public parking lot, which is located off to the left side of the road a short distance beyond the guard station.

## Caneel Bay Plantation

Caneel Bay Plantation was first opened as a resort hotel by the Danish West Indian Company in the 1930s. The property was purchased by Laurance S. Rockefeller in 1952 and underwent an extensive enlargement and improvement program, transforming it into one of the world's premier luxury resorts.

*Equator Restaurant*

After parking your vehicle, you proceed on foot through the exit at the far end of the parking lot.

Directly across the road are the remains of the original sugar plantation. Today the hotel's Equator Restaurant is situated on top of the former horsemill where sugar cane was once crushed for processing.

Caneel Bay Plantation played a dramatic role in the story of the St. John slave revolt. The ruins are thought to be part of the original Durloe Plantation where a small group of planters, fearing for their lives, gathered to defend themselves against attacking rebels. The group was able to hold off the murderous horde just long enough to escape in a boat that arrived from St. Thomas. Although many of the Durloe plantation buildings have disappeared, the foundations of the sugar factory and estate house are thought to be original.

Scattered among the Caneel ruins are many varieties of tropical plants including bananas, limes, breadfruit and flowering bougainvillea. Caneel keeps its vegetation looking green and healthy year round by recycling raw sewage and using the water to irrigate the soil.

*Breadfruit, By Thomas B. Howell*

One of the more exotic specimens on the resort grounds is the lignum vitae (bushy looking tree with orange fruit). There is an example of one growing alongside the remains of the well tower. The wood of the lignum vitae is extremely hard (making it termite resistant). During Danish colonial times, it was frequently used for making fence posts.

When you are ready to depart, return to your vehicle. Retrace your path back to North Shore Road, where you

# Beaches

The following is a list of some of the most popular and accessible beaches and snorkeling spots on St. John: *(See centerfold map, pgs. 74-75, for beach locations.)*

## North Side:

**(1)    Solomon Beach**
Palm-fringed beach with gorgeous white sand. Good snorkeling. Solomon is St. John's unofficial nudist beach. Heading out of Cruz Bay on North Shore Road, turn left at the top of the hill just before reaching the National Park sign. Near the end of the road is a trail leading down to the beach. No facilities.

**(2)    Honeymoon Beach**
Similar in beauty and setting to adjacent Solomon Beach. Lovely sandy beach ideal for swimming and snorkeling. Can be reached via same trail that takes you to Solomon or from Caneel Bay Plantation. Honeymoon Beach has public facilities including changing room and picnic area.

**(3)    Caneel Bay Beach**
Located directly in front of the hotel's main lobby and restaurant is this white sandy beach. It is open to the public. Amenities such as beach

chairs, lounges, towels, etc. are reserved for registered guests.

**(4) Hawksnest Beach**
Popular swimming and snorkeling beach. Attracts locals and visitors alike.

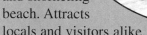

Beautiful white sandy expanse. Water can get rough during winter months. Snorkeling is best along the reefs on the eastern side of the beach. Picnic facilities.

**(5)    Trunk Bay**
Classic St. John beach. Most visited beach and arguably one of the most beautiful beaches on St. John. National Park Services has an underwater snorkel trail with markers identifying sea life. Lifeguard on duty. Restaurant and retail shop. Picnic facilities and restrooms.

**(6)    Cinnamon Bay**
Beautiful, long, white sandy beach with plenty of areas to

get shade from the sun. Beach has many things to do. Besides swimming and snorkeling, visitors can observe the site of a recent archeological dig for Taino Indian artifacts. There is also a nature walk, which passes through the Cinnamon Bay ruins. Additional amenities include a watersports center, snack bar, retail store, restrooms and changing facilities. Lifeguard on duty.

**(7)     Francis Bay Beach**
Lovely sandy beach known for excellent snorkeling as well as swimming. Fun to watch the pelicans dive for their dinner in the bay. Popular anchorage for yachts. Reached via the Francis Bay Trail where you enjoy a pleasurable stroll past ruins of historic Francis Bay Estate House. Bird watchers like observing wildlife in salt pond habitat from the overlook near the estate house.

**(8)     Waterlemon Bay Beach**
Located along Leinster Bay, this is an excellent spot for snorkeling, although the beach itself is rocky. Best snorkeling is around Waterlemon Cay (30 minute walk) at far east end of the beach. Reach the beach on foot after parking your car in paved area below the Annaberg ruins.

## *East End:*
**(1)     Hansen Bay (Vie's Beach)**
Vie's is a great escape and change of pace from most of the other beaches on St. John. A white sandy stretch of sand with sparkling clear water and some good snorkeling. Located opposite Vie's Snack Bar, Vie charges admission for access to the beach. The fare is well worth it. It is very often sunny here, even when it is cloudy and overcast elsewhere on St. John.

## *South Side:*

### (1)    Salt Pond Beach

One of the nicest beaches on the island. Sandy and clear water. Lovely expanse of beach. Opportunity to experience some of St. John's arid vegetation as you walk from the parking area along the path to the beach. Excellent snorkeling. Refreshments usually on sale in parking lot area. No facilities.

### (2)    Lameshur Bay Beach

Nice swimming beach with reasonably good snorkeling at either end of the beach. Opportunity to wander through the ruins of ancient bay rum factory. Picnic area and restrooms.

### (3)    Reef Bay

Remote, gorgeous beach located at the end of Reef Bay Trail. Also reached via car and a not-so-well-known path just past Fish Bay. Find your way to Fish Bay Road and follow to intersection of Marina Drive and Reef Bay Road, where you turn left and proceed up the hill. You go another 0.2 mile and turn left after crossing the section of concrete pavement. A short distance ahead you should locate the path, which begins its decent next to a telephone pole. Ask a neighbor for directions, if you get lost.

continue heading east. A short distance ahead is Hawksnest Beach. Hawksnest is one of several gorgeous swimming beaches located along the north side of the island. Public facilities at Hawksnest include charcoal grills and a picnic area.

Continuing on, a short distance past Hawksnest, you will pass the Gibney-Oppenheimer Beach. This is where the famous scientist, Robert Oppenheimer, once had a home. Robert Oppenheimer, was the inventor of the atomic bomb. Oppenheimer appreciated the refuge the island afforded him, especially after it was rumored that he had been approached by the Soviets and had thus become the object of much scrutiny by the C.I.A. Oppenheimer's house was left to the children of the Virgin Islands by his daughter and is now used as a recreation facility.

Along this stretch of the road there are numerous panoramic vistas of the many surrounding islands. Just before reaching Trunk Bay you will come to a scenic overlook, easily recognized by a stone wall spanning its length. It is a great spot to pull over and take photographs of Trunk Bay Beach, thought by many to be the most beautiful beach on St. John.

*Trunk Bay*

## Trunk Bay Beach and Snorkel Trail

In 1959, the National Park purchased Trunk Bay from the Boulon family, who ran a successful guest house at this location for many years.

Trunk Bay takes its name from the trunk or box turtle that once nested here. Pirates prized the box turtle as a food staple because it could be kept alive on the decks of their ships for many days, until it

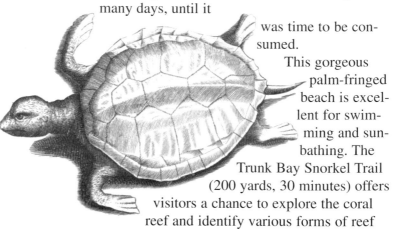

was time to be consumed.

This gorgeous palm-fringed beach is excellent for swimming and sunbathing. The Trunk Bay Snorkel Trail (200 yards, 30 minutes) offers visitors a chance to explore the coral reef and identify various forms of reef life with the aid of a signed underwater trail, which begins near the lifeguard stand.

There is an admission charge, but those paying admission at Trunk can enjoy same day admission to Annaberg (which comes later on in this tour) and vice versa. Children age 16 and under are admitted free; adults, $4.00; individual annual pass, $10.00; family annual pass, $15.00. Golden Age and Golden Access annual cardholders are admitted half price.

Lifeguards are on duty daily. There is a snack bar on the premises. Snorkel gear is available for a small rental fee. Trunk also provides visitors with public telephones, a picnic area and toilets as well as changing and shower facilities.

# Coral Reefs

The warm, clear, shallow waters of the harbors and bays surrounding St. John abound in a variety of colorful coral formations, which provide a home for one of the most diverse and biologically complex ecosystems in the world.

Coral reefs are identified by their overall structure. Two common coral types found around St. John are fringe and barrier coral reefs. Fringe corals ring the shoreline in close and barrier corals run parallel to the shore and are clustered in large masses out further.

Corals are actually tiny animals. Live coral formations are composed of billions of tiny individual coral polyps, which keep dying and repeating themselves on top of their skeletons.

*Portion of illustration By John Dawson, Courtesy National Park Service*

Coral polyps have a cup-shaped body with a single opening at the top, through which they obtain planktonic food and oxygen. Coral polyps build their skeletal structures by secreting calcium carbonate, forming hard cups called corallites. The hard cups protect the soft delicate bodies of the living animal.

*Coral Polyp, Courtesy National Park Service*

The existence of many plants and animals depends on the continued health of the coral reefs, which are threatened by a variety of causes including run-off, sewage, recreational diving and boating, storms, algal blooms and global warming.

Divers and snorkelers are cautioned not to touch coral growth. The simple touch of a human hand can kill whole colonies that took millions of years to grow. Common coral species seen around St. John are:

*Brain*

## Brain Coral

Brain corals belong to a group of corals known as the stony corals. They are part of a subclass of corals called hexacorallia. The stony corals comprise the basic building blocks of coral reefs. The brain coral derives its name from its brain-like appearance.

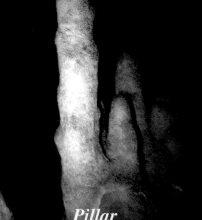

*Pillar*

## Branching and Pillar Coral

Like the brain coral, the branching and pillar corals also belong to the stony or "hard" coral group. The pillar corals grow upward in clusters of heavy, cylindrical spires. Branching corals also grow upward, but their branches are flattened often resembling the familiar horns and antlers of animals such as elk and moose, after which some of them are named.

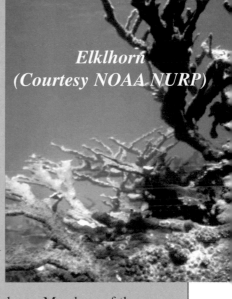

*Elklhorñ*
*(Courtesy NOAA NURP)*

## Sea Whips and Sea Fan

Bushy and feather-like corals that are part of a coral grouping known as gorgonians or "soft corals," because their skeletons do not have a rigid shape. Members of the group include sea fans, sea rods, sea whips and sea plumes. Their tree-like limbs are not calcareous, but are instead composed of a soft rubber-like material. Only the skeletal spicules often visible in the translucent limbs are calcareous. The gor-

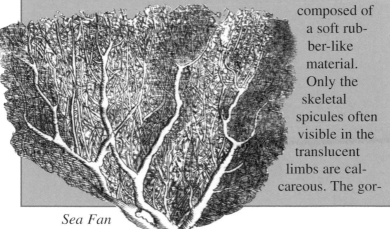

*Sea Fan*

gonians are very beautiful and come in a range of pastel colors. They are usually found clinging to rocks, rubble and reefs.

### Fire Coral

Fire corals belong to a group of corals called hydrocorals. Fire corals will produce a painful burning sensation when touched, so stay clear. They are often mistaken for stony corals. There are several group patterns, including blade coral, branching coral and box fire coral. These corals can be readily identified by their relatively smooth surface. They are generally tan to mustard color in appearance. Fire corals will frequently encrust or "splatter" themselves over other coral colonies.

*Fire Coral Encrusting*

Although most of St. John's underwater creatures are harmless, visitors should, however, swim clear of the sea urchin.

The black thorns of the sea urchin have arrow-like tips that are painful and difficult to extract if they become lodged in one's foot. Lime juice is a local remedy used for dissolving embedded spines.

## Cinnamon Bay

The next stop on your tour is Cinnamon Bay. The campground at Cinnamon Bay was established by the National Park Service in 1964. Campers can select personal accommodations ranging from fully equipped, one-room cottages to bare tent sites. Tents can be rented at the commissary.

The main complex, which houses the commissary and cafeteria, are located just off the parking lot. At the activity desk you can obtain information about weekly events that are open to the public. Typical activities include ranger-guided tours of the Cinnamon Bay ruins, a puppet show about the coral reef, and a rendition of the St. John slave revolt.

Leaving the main complex, head in the direction of the beach. Find your way to the old stone building painted white with red doors at the water's edge. This is the headquarters for an important archaeological excavation of Taino Indian artifacts. The dig site is just east of the building. Park archae-

ologists, with the aid of volunteers, have been conducting the search. It has produced numerous fascinating artifacts, including ancient shells, fish and animal bones, pieces of pottery as well as several zemis. Zemi is the name given to small clay or stone figures depicting Taino deities.

Visitors can view examples of unearthed Taino artifacts on display in the headquarters building. Zemi necklaces and T-shirts are on sale to help raise money to finance the on-going dig.

## Cinnamon Bay Loop Trail

Another highlight of a visit to Cinnamon Bay is the self-guided walking tour of the Cinnamon Bay Loop Trail. The trail winds past the ruins of a sugar factory and takes you on a pleasant hike through the shady forest above Cinnamon Bay. To reach the trail entrance, walk back up the road from the beach. When you arrive back at the commissary, follow the road past the parking lot and amphitheater to North Shore Road, where you turn left. The trail entrance is located on the right hand side of the road about 100 feet ahead.

# Popular Hiking Trails

A variety of hiking trails help connect visitors with the beautiful beaches and bays, rugged mountains, tropical forests, dry cactus woodlands and historic ruins on St. John. The trail entrances are identified by signs, which also indicate their level of climbing difficulty. *(See centerfold map, pgs. 74-75, for trail locations.)*

### Lind Point Trail (1.1 miles, 1 hour)
Connects the National Park Visitor Center at Cruz Bay with Honeymoon Beach at Caneel Bay. Trail ascends 0.4 miles to scenic Lind Point overlook. At 0.7 miles, a side-trail leads to Solomon Beach. Vegetation features open dry forest with cactus scrub environment.

### Cinnamon Loop Trail (0.5 mile, 1 hour)
Shady, signed, history-nature loop trail passes through an old sugar factory, an old Danish cemetery and native tropical trees. Trail begins a few yards east of entrance road into Cinnamon Bay Campground.

### Francis Bay Trail (0.5 miles, 30 minutes)
Begins at the west end of the Mary Creek paved road near Maho Bay Campground. Trail passes through a dry scrub forest, past historic Francis

Bay Estate House and onto the beach. A mangrove forest and brackish pond provide good bird habitat. An area has been cleared for viewing pond bird life.

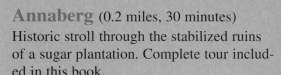

### Annaberg (0.2 miles, 30 minutes)
Historic stroll through the stabilized ruins of a sugar plantation. Complete tour included in this book.

### Salt Pond Trail (0.2 miles, 15 minutes)
Pleasant down hill stroll through arid vegetation to beach at Salt Pond Bay.

### Reef Bay Trail (2.2 miles, 2 hours)
Trail begins 4.9 miles east of Cruz Bay on Centerline Road. It descends through both shady moist and dry forests, both of which incorporate a wide variety of plant life and passes

through several sugar estates along the way. Visit ancient rock carvings ("petroglyphs") made by Taino Indians.

There is a plaque just inside the ruins showing your location and the route of the Cinnamon Bay Loop Trail. It takes about 30 minutes to complete the half-mile course.

Leaving the plaque, walk up the trail about 50 feet to the ruins of the large sugar factory. Note the round circular platform to the left. This is the horsemill where the raw cane stalks were crushed between iron rollers. Power to rotate the rollers was supplied by horses, mules or oxen that were harnessed to a central shaft and forced to walk in a circular path.

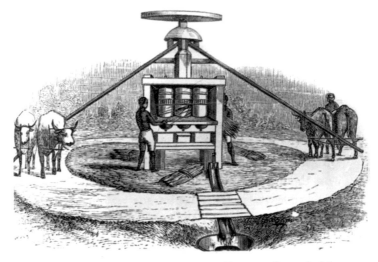

The cane juice extracted from the stalks was funneled by gravity into the factory building where it was heated and boiled in a series of pots. Beds where the pots were seated are still visible on the left side of the ruins.

After exploring the sugar factory, return to the plaque (in front of the factory) and follow the trail along the right hand side of the building. The large circular chimney adjacent to the factory building is attached to several ovens where bread was baked to feed the slaves.

A few steps beyond the factory building, the trail winds to the right and leads to the remains of a bay rum still. The still can be identified by it's pyramidal chimney.

Just to the right of the bay still is a marker indicating the entrance to the hiking trail above the ruins. Before going up the trail, you may want to walk across the small stone bridge to the right where you can view the remains of the Cinnamon Bay Estate House and several out-buildings. The plaque in front of the building shows an artist's rendering of the original estate house. The Cinnamon Bay Estate House was destroyed by a hurricane during the early 1900s, however, the steps leading up to the main entrance are still clearly visible.

Retrace your steps back across the stone bridge, turn right at the bay rum still and head up the path. The surrounding hillsides are dotted with bay trees. Bay trees are easily identified by their smooth brown trunks. The trees thrive in the rich soil and damp climate found on this side of the island. At one time, children were used to climb the trees and pick the leaves and drop them down to women waiting below. The precious oils were extracted and combined with rum and other alco-

holics to make a scented perfume. If you were to crumple a
leaf between your fingers you would immediately experience
the intoxicating and rich aroma of this plant.

About 150 yards past the bay rum still
you come to an old Danish cemetery.
Plantation residents were often buried
in above ground crypts. The size of the
gravestone indicated the economic sta-
tus of the person buried there. Slaves
were usually buried in unmarked
graves along beaches. The largest monument in this cemetery belongs to Anna
Margarethe Berner Hjardamaal whose hus-
band and three sons all died within ten
years of her death. Anna's spouse and
children are buried beside her.

*Bay Trees*

Leaving the cemetery
turn left and continue
walking up the
trail. Along the path
you will pass several
national park plaques
identifying flora and
fauna. Examples of
typical woodland crea-
tures often spotted
along this trail include
zebra butterflies (easily
identified by their zebra-
like markings), wild donkeys, lizards and a variety of birds. If
you listen carefully you can probably identify the eerie cry of
the black witch (smooth-billed anni).

# Animals And Critters

## Mongoose

Furry little rodent-like creatures seen scurrying across roads or along the trails. Brought to St. John from India to rid the island of rats. It did not work, so now we have both! By the way, the plural of mongoose *is*

*Two Mongooses Fighting*

mongooses, not mongeese. The mongoose has no natural enemy on St. John.

## Bats

Plenty of them! Nocturnal airborne mammals that help pollinate the flowering and fruit-bearing trees on St. John. Harmless.

## Hermit (Soldier) Crabs

Creepy, crawly little creatures that doggedly haul shell-houses around on their backs. Heard tumbling down hillsides as they make their way to the seashore where they mate and lay eggs.

## Deer

Wild deer can be found in various parts of the island such as at Calabash Boom and Lameshur Bay.

## No-see-ums

Pesky (nearly invisible) little insects that ferociously attack your legs and feet at the beach. Bite marks generally disappear quickly, but they are a genuine nuisance.

## Iguana

Prehistoric looking reptile of greenish coloring sometimes seen lounging in the sun on the tree branches at Maho Campground. Limited numbers. Very mild-tempered.

## Lizard

Numerous on St. John. Lizards are particularly helpful since they eat mosquitoes, which are plentiful in the evening. Can be seen scurrying up walls and tree trunks. Male lizards display a reddish pouch or dewlap to show territoriality. That combined with a series of "push-ups" warns off competing males and attracts females.

## Millipede

Identified by its long black body and seemingly thousands of tiny legs. The millipede secretes a substance that can cause blindness or skin irritation, but can also be used as a tooth-ache remedy.

One of the first plaques you come to after leaving the cemetery identifies a **TERMITE NEST** *(see photo under Reef Bay Trail, pg. 109)*. You have to look closely up into the trees in order to spot the dark brown mass, which is their nest.

Further on you come to a plaque describing the **ROCK TERRACES** that once rimmed the surrounding hillsides, now overgrown with a dense growth of plants and trees. Terracing was done with slave labor and was designed to make the steep hillsides suitable for crop cultivation.

A few yards ahead, the path dips down and crosses a "gut" or natural streambed. Guts run intermittently, depending upon rainfall. Some guts on St. John have spring fed pools, which once supplied water for livestock. The huge trees with the large green leaves growing along the edge of the gut are **MAMMEE APPLES**. Mammee trees produce a large brown fruit that is used to make jams and preserves. Careful! Don't point. According to local legend "if you point at the fruit of a tree mon, it be shore to pop down on yo head."

Continue following the trail up and out of the gut. The path now starts to wind down the hill on the opposite side of the gut.

Walking on, you come to a plaque identifying the **MANGO TREE**. The fruit of the mango matures between March and October. The mango is best peeled and then eaten raw, stewed or as a preserve. Some people have allergic reactions to the flower or skin of the mango since the fruit is distantly related to poison ivy.

*Indian Picking Mangoes, Artist Unknown*

Look for the plaque picturing the **GOLDEN ORB SPIDER**, which is quite common along this trail. The golden orb is a non-poisonous spider that spends a great deal of energy spinning webs in trees and across paths. The spider is a member of the orb-weaver family and some of his cousins weave webs so strong that the fibers can actually be used to make fish-nets and bags.

Next you will find a plaque identifying the remains of a former **CHARCOAL PIT**. Charcoal was important to early St. Johnians who used it for cooking their meals in coal pot ovens. The "ovens" were open-air cooking stoves that sat about 15" off the table and sort of resembled modern-day fondue pots. These pots were heated by charcoal, which burned underneath them.

Charcoal was manufactured by stacking selected hard-wood saplings and other vegetation in a mound, covering it all with earth, and then lighting the mound on fire. The wood would smolder and become charcoal. The islanders' Sunday "go-to-church" clothes were often kept pressed using an iron called the "goose," which used hot burning coals for heat.

**SWEET LIMES** are identified on a plaque near the end of the trail. This spiny shrub is an invasive plant. It forms thickets in the more recently disturbed moist forests. When in bloom, the white flowers smell like orange blossoms. The sweet lime can be cooked and then the liquid that is extracted can be mixed with sugar to produce a refreshing beverage or food additive. This sticky fruit was once used as a glue substitute.

A few feet further and we emerge at the ruins of the Cinnamon Bay Estate House where the trail ends.

## Moving Along

Return to your car. After leaving the parking lot, turn left on North Shore Road. A few feet beyond the ruins that you just visited, you pass the entrance to the Cinnamon Bay Hiking Trail. Many of the trails on St. John are actually part of the original Danish road system. During colonial times, North Shore Road did not exist. The main thoroughfare was Konge Vej. It traversed the mountaintop and ran between Cruz Bay and Coral Bay, approximating present-day Centerline Road. To reach plantations on the north side, trails such as the Cinnamon Bay Trail ran down the mountainside.

A short distance past Cinnamon, the road passes along the shores of Maho Bay. Maho Bay is a favorite spot for boaters. The beach is excellent for swimming and is conveniently

*Sea Grapes*

located at the edge of the road. You may wish to stop and hunt for sea grapes that grow along the beach.

About a quarter of a mile from Maho Bay, you come to a fork in the road, where you bear left. Just past the fork, look for the preserved remains of an old Danish road on your right. This remnant is part of a road that once connected the neighboring estates of Windberg and Frederiksdal.

A short distance ahead the road splits again. To the left is Francis Bay and the Maho Bay Camps. Go right and continue following the road along Leinister Bay in the direction of the Annaberg ruins.

Driving along the shore, you pass groves of poisonous manchineel trees. Contact with the tree should be avoided as its leaves, bark and tiny green "apples" contain a highly caustic sap. Early explorers recorded numerous bad experiences with the tree. Columbus described its green fruit as "death apples" when several of his men fell critically ill after eating them. In 1526, Gonzalo Fernandez de Oviedo writing in his *Natural History of the West Indies*, described the effects of the fruit as follows: "I say that if a man lies down to sleep for only an hour in the shade of one of these manchineel trees, he awakes with his head and eyes swollen, his

*Manchineel "Apples"*

eyebrows level with his cheeks. If by chance a drop of dew falls from this tree into a man's eyes, his eyes will burst, or at least the man will go blind."

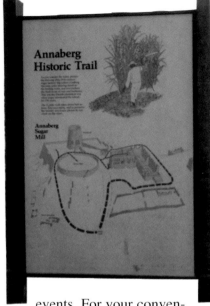

The paved road ends at the entrance to the Annaberg Ruins. Public parking is generally available in the paved area at the bottom of the hill. *(See Trunk Bay for Admission fees.)* The National Park conducts cooking and craft demonstrations at Annaberg. Check with the Visitor Center in Cruz Bay for a schedule of events. For your convenience, the following tour of the Annaberg ruins has been adapted from the Eastern National Park and Monument Association's folder on Annaberg.

## Annaberg Ruins

Annaberg was probably built shortly before 1780. One of her first recorded owners (according to early tax records dating back to 1786) was Benjamin Lind. Lind was a very wealthy man who spent most of his time on his plantation in St. Thomas, trusting the management of Annaberg to an overseer. Down through the years most of Annaberg's owners have been "absentee owners" preferring to live elsewhere, which probably explains why an estate house was never built on the property. In 1816, Annaberg was sold to Thomas and

Mary Sheen and in 1827 it was auctioned off to Hans Henrik Berg, another wealthy St. Thomas resident. Following Berg, there was a succession of owners until the estate was finally purchased by the Virgin Islands National Park in 1956. The National Park stabilized the ruins and restored many of the buildings. The windmill is considered to be one of the largest in the Virgin Islands.

To best explore the Annaberg ruins, follow the trail that begins to the left of the parking lot, stopping at each of the numbered markers along the way.

**(1)    SLAVE QUARTERS**- The first stop on your tour of the ruins is one of sixteen slave cabins found in the area. With a lime concrete floor and a door at one end, each cabin housed a slave family or served as a bachelor quarters. Posts were set in the masonry walls and branches were woven to form wattle that was daubed with a lime and mud mixture. The roof was probably thatched with palm leaves.

(2)     **THE VILLAGE**- On the slope below this wall are the ruins of the slaves' main village site. The women did some of their cooking at a small oven within the village. Slaves grew their own fruits and vegetables on part of the land. Thriftier slaves sold excess food and saved the money to buy their freedom.

It is often difficult for us to imagine how hard life must have been for a slave. The misery began from the moment he or she was sold into bondage. Conditions were so bad on some slave ships that slaves were lucky to survive the crossing. Once here, slaves next had to face the denigration of the auction block. "At that time," wrote Virgin Islands historian, Antonio Jarvis in his book, *Brief History of the Virgin Islands*, "slave auctions were the most exciting event of any month. When the slaver entered the port, the white inhabitants rushed to the water's edge and took to boats in order to get a preview of the living cargo....Despite the unholy stench, and the ravages of filth from such a voyage, the partly washed freight tried to put on a look of complacence, save where some untamed chieftain in lofty tones demanded his release, or a hysterical woman alternately screamed or sobbed."

"When the slaves were finally put ashore and marched to the auction block," Jarvis continued, "a huge crowd of prospective buyers, sailors, prostitutes and free blacks with earrings and store clothes, gathered to see the sale. Lascivious men fingered the merchandise more for pleasure than for profit, and the women had to suffer the degradation of being minutely examined in public. Their breasts were felt and pulled, mouths looked into, their buttocks slapped, and their very tribal marks were objects of close scrutiny."

Once purchased and placed on plantations, harsh laws and cruel treatment were the slaves' daily bread. Public beatings were a common occurrence. Any good-looking black girl was fair game for a master's carnal appetite.

(3)     **BAGASSE**- The crushed stock of sugar cane. The stock was dried and stored in sheds to be used as fuel. These stone columns are all that remain of the shed at Annaberg.

(4)     **IMAGINE**- All the slopes above you covered with cane. With a short handled knife the slaves cut the cane, stripped the leaves, and tied the stock into bundles. Then, loading the bundles on a mule or cart, they hauled the cane to Annaberg for processing.

(5)     **WINDMILL**- If a steady wind blew, the cane was brought to the windmill to be crushed. Revolving sails turned a central shaft that rotated the rollers, crushing the stalks. Juice then ran down the rollers to the gutter and flowed by gravity to the factory. The wooden structure visible inside the windmill carried the axle and sails and could be turned into the wind.

(6)     **HORSEMILL**- The wind was not always dependable. In calm weather cane stalks were crushed on this circular horsemill. Here the mules, oxen or horses were harnessed to poles and plodded around the circular course, turning the upright iron rollers in the center of the platform. Slaves passed the cane between the rollers, which crushed the stalks

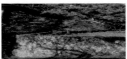

and released the juices.

**(7)    BOILING BENCH**- Coming through a hole in the wall directly above the boiling bench, the cane juice flowed into the first of five coppers (iron kettles). Fires fed with dried cane stalks heated the coppers from beneath. Workers added lime and brought the juices to a boil, evaporating some of the water. After skimming off the impurities, they ladled the juice

from one copper to the next. From the last and smallest copper they poured the concentrated and purified juice into flat wooden pans to cool, crystallize and drain off excess moisture. Once the crystals had formed, the sugar was placed in large wooden barrels (called hogsheads) to be thoroughly dried and stored.

**(8)    DRIPPINGS CISTERN**- Workers stored the hogsheads of wet sugar on trestles in back rooms of the factory. Liquid drippings from the hogsheads funneled into the cistern on the right in the room below. The owners used this sweet liquid to produce rum. They wasted nothing.

**(9)    WATER CISTERN**- A great quantity of water was needed to produce sugar and to support the people living and working on the estate. As ground water was not readily available, rainwater from the roof flowed through the gutters into this cistern. The cistern holds about 20,000 gallons.

**(10)     OVEN**- Most of the estate's bread was baked in this oven. The baker filled the large chamber with wood and char-

coal, then lighted it. When only the hot coals remained, he raked the embers through the grating into the ash box below. Dough placed in the hot oven soon sent the delicious aroma of baking bread through the air.

**(11)     DUNGEON**- A chain and pair of handcuffs were found fastened to a post in the left corner of this small chamber, making the room's use as a dungeon a good guess. The drawings of schooners and the street scene may well date back to Danish times.

**(12)     SUGAR APPLES**- The small trees along this part of the path are sugar apples, one of the many plants available to the slaves for food. The sweet pulp of the large green apple is eaten raw or used to prepare drinks.

**(13)    BUILDING MATERIALS**- Notice the rough fragments of volcanic rock used in the construction of this building. The rocks are set in a mortar consisting of sand, fresh water, molasses and lime. Where arches and corners called for square or special shaped stones, both coral and bricks were used. Brain coral was very popular because it could be cut and shaped easily when it was first taken from the sea and was still soft. Red and yellow bricks came from Europe as ballast on ships.

**(14)    STORAGE ROOM**- This room and the one to the right were used to store sugar and to age rum before shipment to North American and European markets.

**(15)    RUM STILL**- This platform once supported the factory's rum still. Here, above a slow fire, workers placed the fermented molasses into a copper still. Copper tubing then led the alcohol vapors from the still to a cistern located behind it. There the coils of copper, immersed in cool water, converted the vapors to rum. The raw rum, or kill devil, was piped into casks located in the adjacent room.

**(16)    LIME TREE**- Limes came to the New World more than 400 years ago. The fruit makes a refreshing drink and the leaves of the tree can be used to brew a delicious bush tea.

**(17)    FIRING TUNNELS**- Here slaves fed bagasse to the fire that heated the boiling bench above. At one time a chimney was located near this post. It provided the draft necessary to pull the fire into the tunnels and under the coppers.

**(18)    OX POUND**- Though we call it the ox pound, mules

were most commonly used for work (along with horses and donkeys) on sugar plantations.

This completes your tour of Annaberg. The last two stops on the North Shore tour will be Francis Bay and the Maho Bay Camps. Return to your vehicle and retrace your steps to the intersection at the other end of Leinster Bay. Bear to the right at the intersection, and continue following the road along the water's edge until reaching the entrance (on the right hand side of the road) to the Francis Bay Trail. The entrance to the trail is marked by the presence of an old warehouse, bearing the inscription of two dates: 1814 and 1911.

## Francis Bay Trail

The Francis Bay Trail is 0.5 miles in length and takes about 30 minutes to walk. It is a pleasant, relatively easy stroll through dry scrub forest, past the remains of an old estate house (about 20 yards from the entrance to the trail) and onto the beach.

Just past the old estate house is an observation area that is kept clear for unobstructed viewing of birds. The mangrove forest and brackish salt pond below provide a favorable habitat. There are 160 birds that appear on the National Park's checklist of birds, which can be found on St. John. Many of the birds can be seen at this location. Visitors wanting to learn more about St. John's bird life, may wish to sign-up for a park service bird-watching tour.

# Birds

The bird population on St. John is large and diverse. Many birds are indigenous to the West Indies and many others migrate to the West Indies from North America during the winter months. Here are some of the more common permanent residents:

**Hummingbirds**

**Heron**

**Bananaquits**

**Pelicans**

The observation area affords a good view of the bay. The area just south of Francis Bay is Little Maho Bay, former home of Ethel McCully. Ms. McCully is one of St. John's many colorful past residents. She resided at Little Maho Bay in a house that she designed herself and had constructed in the days when donkeys were the main means of transporting building materials. Ms.McCully fell instantly in love with St. John upon viewing it for the first time from the deck of a boat headed for Tortola. She immediately informed the captain that she was getting off, dove over the side, and swam ashore. For many years, Ms McCully enjoyed life in her St. John home, which she named "Island Fancy," before selling it to the National Park shortly before her death. Ms McCully's book, *Grandma Raised the Roof*, in which she details many of her fascinating island adventures, is out of print, but can be found at the library in town.

Swimming and snorkeling are favorite activities at Francis Bay. If you decide to go for a swim, avoid the deep-water passage off Mary Point where there are often strong currents and heavy boat traffic.

When leaving the beach, retrace your steps back up the trail, and return to your vehicle. Drive a few yards further down the road, turn left, and follow the sign to Maho Bay Camps.

## Maho Bay Camps

Maho Bay Camps is an environmentally sensitive luxury campground offering affordable accommodations to those wishing to experi-

ence St. John's natural beauty close-up. This "green" resort was conceived and built by pioneer eco-resort developer, Stanley Selengut, in the 1970s. The resort was constructed using techniques that caused minimal erosion, thereby avoiding coral reef damage. Mr. Selengut was well ahead of the times with his efforts to preserve the ecology of this popular tourist destination.

Maho's tent dwellings are connected by wooden walkways perched above the land and each is equipped with a cooking area and icebox. Maho uses alternative energy sources wherever possible and encourages visitors to recycle and reuse consumer products. A glass reclamation workshop is located on the premises and is open to visitors on Fridays. Some of the items made at the workshop, such as floor tiles, are used at the camp. Other small items such as sun-catchers, candle

*Glass Blowing Demonstration*

sticks and pitchers are sold at the Maho Bay store, which also sells assorted grocery items and is a good place to get a cold drink or snack.

A variety of day and evening events, well worth noting, are posted on the blackboard at the restaurant. These events are usually free and generally include lectures and slide shows, as well as musical performances. Sailing, snorkeling, wind-surfing and diving lessons are offered between 9:00 a.m. - 4:00 p.m. daily. Other activities, including island tours, yoga classes, boating adventures and assorted day trips are also offered. Ask for a copy of the "What's Happening at Maho" schedule at the Activities Booth,

*Air Plant*

which is open daily from 8:00 a.m.-1:00 p.m. and 4:00 p.m.-7:00 p.m.

***This concludes the North Side Tour.***

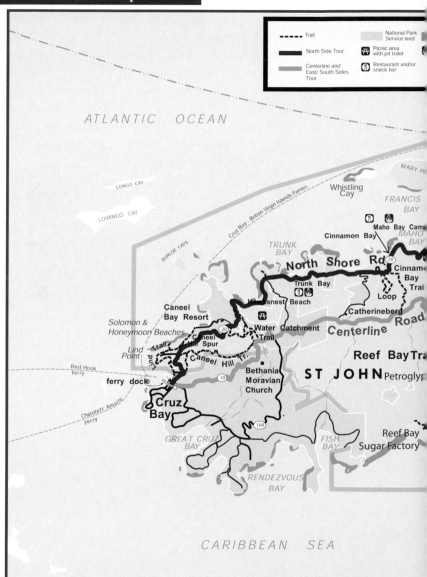

Trail

North Side Tour

Centerline and East/ South Sides Tour

National Park Service land

Picnic area with pit toilet

Restaurant and/or snack bar

ATLANTIC OCEAN

CONGO CAY

LOVANGO CAY

DURLOE CAYS

Cruz Bay - British Virgin Islands Ferries

Whistling Cay

MARY P

FRANCIS BAY

Maho Bay Camp

MAHO BAY

Cinnamon Bay

TRUNK BAY

North Shore Rd

Cinnam Bay Trai

Trunk Bay

Hawksnest Beach

Loop

Catherineberg

Centerline Road

Caneel Bay Resort

Water Catchment Trail

Solomon & Honeymoon Beaches

Caneel Hill Spur

Reef Bay Tra

Lind Point

Caneel Hill Tr.

ST JOHN Petroglyp

Red Hook Ferry

Trail

Bethania Moravian Church

ferry dock

Charolett Amalie Ferry

Cruz Bay

GREAT CRUZ BAY

FISH BAY

Reef Bay Sugar Factory

RENDEZVOUS BAY

CARIBBEAN SEA

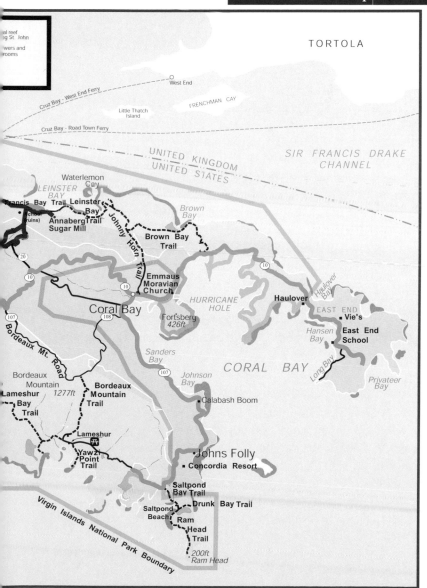

TORTOLA

O West End

Cruz Bay - West End Ferry

Little Thatch
Island

FRENCHMAN CAY

Cruz Bay - Road Town Ferry

UNITED KINGDOM
UNITED STATES

SIR FRANCIS DRAKE
CHANNEL

LEINSTER
BAY

Waterlemon
Cay

Francis Bay Trail   Leinster
Bay

Brown
Bay

(School
ruins)

Annaberg Trail
Sugar Mill

Johnny Horn Trail

Brown Bay
Trail

20

10

10

Emmaus
Moravian
Church

Haulover Bay

10

Coral Bay

107

108

HURRICANE
HOLE

Haulover

EAST END

Vie's

Bordeaux Mt. Road

Fortsberg
426ft

Hansen
Bay

East End
School

Long Bay

Bordeaux
Mountain

1277ft

Bordeaux
Mountain
Trail

Lameshur
Bay
Trail

Sanders
Bay

107

Johnson
Bay

CORAL   BAY

Privateer
Bay

Calabash Boom

Lameshur

Yawzi
Point
Trail

Johns Folly

Concordia  Resort

Saltpond
Bay Trail

Drunk Bay Trail

Saltpond
Beach

Ram
Head
Trail

Virgin Islands National Park Boundary

200ft
Ram Head

# Centerline Including East End and South Side

## Getting Started

Centerline Road (Route 10) actually begins at the fork where the Texaco Gas Station in Cruz Bay is located. It is the road to the left of the gas station. Starting up Centerline you may begin to notice changes in the vegetation. As you climb higher and higher, the plant life becomes more dense and lush. St. John offers a wide variation in tropical vegetation due to the differing amounts of rain that fall across the island. The south and east shores are considerably drier than the north shore and mountaintops. The latter often receive more than 70 inches of rain a year! During late fall, the cow pastures along Centerline are ablaze with the soft, blue petals of morning glories.

About a mile from the Texaco station, you will come to a concrete road on the right leading to the Bethania Moravian Church.

## Bethania Moravian Church

Moravians and Lutherans were the only groups originally permitted by the Danes to set up churches in the Virgin Islands. Eventually, Anglicans, Dutch-Reformed, Catholics, Jews and other religious groups were also allowed to conduct worship.

Arriving on St. John in 1783, the Moravians set up two missions, one here at Bethania and a second, Emmaus, in Coral Bay. Schools were established and slaves were taught how to read and write. Moravian missionaries were excellent craftsmen. They taught their skills to the slaves during

# Flowers of St. John

**Bougainvilla**

At various times of the year, the hillsides of St. John burst forth in a dazzling array of beautiful flowering plants, trees and bushes.

**Frangipani (Garden Variety)**

**Hibiscus**

**Frangipani (Wild)**

**Ginger Thomas**
*Official Flower of the Virgin Islands*

evening hours after regular chores on the plantations were

done. When public education came into effect with the passage of a School Ordinance in 1827, Moravians continued to play an important role as teachers and administrators in the public school system.

With the exception of the belfry (a recent addition, dating 1919), the present day church was part of the original Bethania Mission.

Interesting structures found on the grounds include the parish hall (a recent renovation of an 18th-century building), the vaulted cistern behind

the parish hall and the little house behind the church with its two Danish ovens.

Leaving the Moravian Church, turn right onto Centerline (East 10). Continue driving east toward Coral Bay. Watch out for farm livestock that occasionally wanders (and naps!) along this stretch of the road. Approximately 2 miles ahead is the road leading to Estate Cathrineberg on your left. The road is identified by a marker pointing in the direction of Route 206.

## Estate Cathrineberg

A short distance up the road, you arrive first at the crumbling ruins of several factory buildings on your left. Next you reach the circular horsemill, followed by the well-preserved

ruins of the Cathrineberg windmill.

Estate Cathrineberg is one of the oldest plantations on St. John. The first recorded owner was Andreas Hammer who filed the original land grant in 1724. In place of the conventional solid foundation found beneath most windmills, there is instead a round vaulted room.

Leaving the windmill, retrace your path to Centerline Road, and turn left. About a mile and a half beyond Cathrineberg, you will come to an overlook with a national park marker identifying the surrounding islands. This is an excellent spot for taking photographs.

# Getting Our Bearings

As the plaque explains, the island to the right, just beyond Mary's Point, is Tortola. Straight ahead is Whistling Cay. Just beyond Whistling Cay comes Jost Van Dyke, named after a Dutch pirate. Many well-known pirates achieved their fame in these waters. Captain Kidd was actually hanged a few miles from here on St. Thomas. The drawings of pirate ships on the dungeon walls at Annaberg bear witness to the former presence of these seafaring rogues.

Driving on, you will eventually notice a sign marking the entrance to the Reef Bay Trail, after which the road rises up to a spectacular overlook located adjacent to the Chateau

Bourdeaux restaurant. Stop and enjoy the view. The wide body of water on the left side of St. John is Drake's Passage.

The road to the right of the overlook leads to the top of Bordeaux Mountain, which is mentioned here as an optional side trip. The Bordeaux road can be quite rough at certain times of the year and is definitely not recommended for vehicles not equipped with 4-wheel drive.

## Bordeaux Mountain (optional)

Bordeaux Mountain is the highest spot on St. John, rising 1,277 feet above sea level. The Bordeaux Mountain road winds through groves of bay trees, and eventually reaches a tiny settlement where St. John's bay leaf pickers once lived. During the early 1900s, the bay tree gave St. John her most important industry, the manufacture of bay oil. Workers would comb the mountainside picking bay leaves that were then loaded on donkeys and hauled to the bay still at

### Donkeys

Wild donkeys are very common on St. John. Watch out when driving or walking down trails. They often appear quite unexpectedly. Donkeys were once the principal means of transportation on the island. Now they roam freely and often cause lots of mischief by digging up gardens and upsetting campsites. It is perfectly okay to snap photographs from a safe distance, but do not attempt to pet or feed these animals. Remember, they are "wild" and are often not quite as friendly as they may appear. It is not at all uncommon for one to attempt to bite or kick an unsuspecting visitor.

# Rastafarians

Rastafarians (or "Rastas") are a growing presence on St. John and throughout the Caribbean. Their long hair, braided in dreadlocks, is a familiar trademark. Rasta followers are often associated with the backbeat sound of reggae music, which has become an international phenomenon made popular by singers such as Bob Marley and Jimmy Cliff.

Rastafarianism is an Ethiopian-based religion in which Haile Selassie (1892-1974) is regarded as the everlasting God, or JAH, whose spirit lives on in practicing Rastafarians today. Followers of the Rastafari movement believe Haile Selassie, whose real name was Ras Tafari Makonnem, to be a descendant of King Solomon and the Queen of Sheba. As emperor (ca.1930-74), Haile Selassie was responsible for implementing many reforms aimed at improving the plight of his people.

Rastafarianism is dedicated to the opposition of oppression and preservation of nature. Marijuana (or Ganja") plays a key role in the Rastafari lifestyle and is used for spiritual and medicinal purposes.

Lameshur Bay. At Lameshur the leaves were boiled in seawater to extract the richly scented oil. The oil was then packed in barrels and shipped to St. Thomas where it was mixed with alcohol, producing cologne.

The rich soil and damp climate create an ideal environment for many plants, making it the area of choice for members of

St. John's Rastafarian religion who are actively involved with the cultivation of indigenous plants on St. John.

## Moving Along

Departing the overlook, you begin your twisting descent down the mountainside into Coral Bay. Along this route you will find several spots to stop and admire the panoramic views. Look carefully toward

*Papaya Tree*

the center of the valley. Try and spot the remains of the windmill at Estate Caroline, buried deep in the bush.

The windmill is on private land and cannot be visited without permission of the owners.

## Coral Bay

Coral Bay is the site of the first Danish settlement on St. John. "Here," recalls Governor Bredel in a letter to Copenhagen in 1717, the Danish West India and Guinea Company "planted the flag of our most gracious King, fired a salute, and then feasted and drank health, first of our Sovereign and then the Company." Initially the settlement grew rapidly. The future of Coral Bay seemed promising. But when the sugar economy collapsed, Coral Bay lost a great deal of its original purpose. Gradually, Cruz Bay became the logical principal port because of its close proximity to St. Thomas.

In recent years, Coral Bay has experienced a small resurgence in popularity, especially among the boating community, which is well aware of the harbor's historic reputation as a safe anchorage. A portion of the harbor is actually referred to as Hurricane Hole, because of the excellent protection it offers boats during these menacing storms.

One of the more intriguing sites in Coral Bay (which is not accessible to visitors) is the location of the fortress known as Fort Berg. This is the actual spot where the slave revolt of 1733-34 began. The fort was situated atop the large cone-shaped hill on the far left hand side of the harbor. The original stockade was improved during the British occupation of 1807-14. It held as many as eighteen guns.

*Fort Berg Battery*
*By Thomas B. Howell*

# Moravians

Missionaries of the Moravian Church, who began arriving in the Virgin Islands in 1732, played an extremely important role in the religious instruction and general education of the black population under Danish sovereignty

In the begining, the planters were very suspicious of the Moravians who often showed a deep dislike for harsh punishment. The St. John slave revolt had made them very fearful of anything that threatened to undermine a social order that trusted only submissive slaves.

Gradually, the missionaries gained the trust of the planters who began to see some benefit in the Christian message, which they interpreted as emphasizing one's duty to faithfully and unquestioningly serve one's master.

Chapels were built and blacks were allowed to come together for meetings and worship. Attending the missions was appealing to the slaves who were generally not allowed to talk with each other during the weekdays and were rarely allowed out in the evenings. The missions gave the slaves a sense of self-

respect. By successfully completing certain steps in a prescribed learning process, slaves could show themselves worthy of baptism and could also work their way up through various positions within the church.

Moravians insisted that their missionaries be trained as artisans so they could support themselves. This notion was passed on to the members of their black congregations, many of whom became skilled carpenters, stone masons, coopers and basket makers. These skills played an important role in the survival of the local population after Emancipation and the collapse of the plantation system.

## Emmaus Moravian Church

At the heart of Coral Bay is the Emmaus Moravian Church (large yellow structure with red roof) set against the hillside across from the park as you enter the settlement. The Emmaus Moravian Church was constructed during the

late 1700s. Although most historical accounts say that the location of the original great house of the Carolina Plantation was at the upper end of the valley in Coral Bay, some sources contend that the Emmaus Church and parish hall are actually built on the foundations of the spot where Judge Sodtmann and his daughter were murdered during the historic slave revolt. Local superstition suggests that the church grounds may be haunted by their spirits.

Leaving the church, go left onto Route 10. The road eventually winds its way to the extreme eastern portion of St. John, a relatively remote area referred to locally as "East End."

*"The Haulover" Bridge*

## East End

East End is geographically defined as all the land east of "The Haulover," which basically begins at the little concrete bridge located about one-tenth of a mile past Estate Zootenvaal. "The Haulover" takes its name from the fact that area residents once used nearby Haulover Bay as a launching point for their boats.

Before construction of Centerline Road, East End was an extremely isolated and sparsely populated area. In 1835, the East End population totaled only 222 people (107 whites, 79 slaves and 36 free blacks). Following Emancipation, the population declined steadily: in 1870 — 143 people, in 1917 — 113 people and by 1938, there were only 78 souls living on East End.

Except for an annual boat trip to pay taxes at the Administration Building in Cruz Bay, most East End residents had little contact with the rest of St. John. The isolation of the area fostered a strong sense of independence. Members of the community worked together on projects both collectively and in small groups called "clubs" in order to survive. East Enders supported themselves through trades such as charcoal making, fishing, boat building, stone masonry, basketry and lime production.

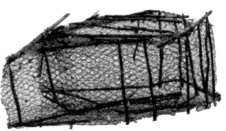

*Local Fish Trap*

During the plantation period, East End was divided into three distinct estates: Hermitage, Retreat (also referred to as Perfect) and Haulover (not to be confused with "The Haulover" discussed above). Because of the area's dry and arid climate, the East End estates were not used for production of sugar and cotton as was the case elsewhere on St. John. Instead, they were used largely for cattle and livestock raising.

Free blacks tended to congregate on the non-productive estates of East End as well as on some of the poorer land south of Coral Bay. Areas like John's Folly and Hard Labor, as their names imply, were not highly regarded by white planters and were generally ignored and left for slaves and black freemen to use for gardening and raising animals.

Water was a precious and scarce commodity on East End. Residents who lived here during the late 18th- and early 19th-century lived primarily in a dozen tiny houses clustered up the hillside along the "gut" (stream-bed) above Hansen Bay.

# Basketry

Basket making was at one point an important industry on St. John. The fine quality and beauty of St. John baskets was world-renowned.

Basically, two types of baskets were produced from plants that grow here: hoop and wist. Sturdy hoop baskets were fashioned from the hoop vine *(Trichostigma octandrum)* and wist baskets from the wist reed *(Serjania polyphylla)*, a much more delicate plant. Generally, women made wist baskets and men made hoop baskets.

Wist baskets were used for household items such as placemats, sewing baskets, flowerpots, breadbaskets and cup holders. Hoop baskets were used for luggage, cargo, and market baskets.

Basket making is an extremely labor intensive task. The process of gathering the hoop and wist was very time consuming, as was the

*Ralph Prince, Expert Local Basket Weaver*

actual process of making baskets, one of which could take anywhere from 3-7 days to construct.

In the early 1900s, St. John basketry formed an important part of the local economy. It gave the people an important cash source from which to buy things they did not raise, grow or catch in the sea. St. John baskets were originally sold from the decks of schooners on St. Croix and St. Thomas. In the 1930s, they were marketed through a co-operative on St. Thomas and later to tourists who arrived on cruise ships.

*Author's Note: Much of the information currently available about the importance and history of basketry on St. John comes from the tireless efforts of Dr. Bernard A. Kemp, an economist and eminent researcher who has spent many years in residence on St. John.*

Cooking was done outdoors over coal pot stoves. Water was collected in barrels, which drained from roof-tops and wells. The well water was brackish, and used principally for feeding livestock. Inadequate water supply resulted in the outbreak of a deadly typhoid epidemic in 1903-04. The epidemic was eventually stamped out thanks to the compassion and generosity of the Moravian Church, which financed the construction of a new community cistern (completed in 1907) next to the school at White Bay. The only other East End cistern in existence at the time was privately owned.

## East End Checklist

As you explore the East End community, here are some local sights to look for:

## ROBERTS CISTERN

The Roberts Cistern was constructed in 1907 and was privately owned. As you travel east, you can spot it located on the hillside near the road just a few yards before Vie's Snack Bar. Water was extremely important to East End residents for drinking and cooking (especially in preparing soups and in steaming fish) and had to be used sparingly. Most early East End families limited themselves to a gallon a day!

## SCHOOL AND CISTERN

The East End School is prominently perched on a hilltop overlooking White Bay, a short distance from Vie's. The school was constructed in 1862 and closed in 1960. For a short while, it was used as the summer house for the lieutenant governor of the Virgin Islands. The school was originally built on private property, which was subsequently transferred to the Moravian Church in 1913. Moravians continued to teach at the school even after it was made public under U.S. ownership of the island. The school roof was blown off in a hurricane in 1924, and it had to be replaced with assistance from the local government. This was one of the rare occasions that

*East End School
and Community Cistern*

the self-reliant East End community felt the need to reach out beyond its community borders for help.

    The community cistern, discussed earlier, is located between the school and the road. The cistern was completed in 1907 and is generally credited with saving the community from a typhoid epidemic. It was built under the guidance and direction of Reverend Foster, who was pastor at the time of the Emmaus Moravian Church in Coral Bay. You will find Reverend Foster's name and the date of completion inscribed above the cistern door.

### PRIVATEER BAY

This picturesque bay is located at the very tip of the East End peninsula. It takes its name from ancient sea rovers who would stop here to rest and repair their ships. It is a commonly held belief that a great deal of pirate treasure may be buried along these shores. The hillsides and area around Privateer Bay have been subdivided into residential lots. The views from the hilltops are magnificent! Clearly visible are Tortola off to the left followed by Peter Island (straight ahead) and Norman Island to the right. You arrive at Privateer Bay by following the dirt road, which leads off to the left (look for the mail boxes!), just before the main road ends at Long Bay.

*Privateer Bay*

# Pirates and Treasure

Notorious pirates like Edward Teach ("Blackbeard"), Captain Kidd and Jean Hamil once freely plied the waters and bays around St. John. Pirates came here hoping to plunder gold and silver from passing galleons.

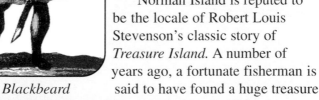

There is lots of talk about buried treasure in the Virgin Islands. In actuality, most pirates being impetuous souls, probably spent the bulk of their booty on gambling, women and other pleasures almost as quickly as it was acquired. Yet the rumors persist!

Norman Island is reputed to be the locale of Robert Louis Stevenson's classic story of *Treasure Island.* A number of years ago, a fortunate fisherman is said to have found a huge treasure

*Blackbeard*

of Spanish doubloons in a cave on Norman Island.

The fisherman's treasure may have been part of a large cargo of gold and silver stolen from the Spanish merchant ship, *La Nuestra Senora de la Guadeloupe*, which went aground off the coast of North Carolina in 1750. According to the records, *La Nuestra Senora's* treasure was illicitly diverted to the Virgin Islands by a

couple of untrustworthy captains who were charged with off-loading it in North Carolina.

Somehow the unscrupulous captains managed to find their way to the Virgin Islands where they met an equally untrustworthy local sea captain by the name of Norman. He helped them hide the doubloons (in exchange for a sizeable cut!) on Liberty Island, which eventually assumed his name. The three thieves were apprehended and appropriately punished by Spanish authorities. They never got to enjoy their wealth. Most of the treasure was eventually recovered from Norman Island where it was found buried in numerous locations.

*Pirates Attacking Spanish Ship From John Exquemelin, ca 1700*

## Beaches and Bays

East End bays like White Bay, Long Bay, Hansen Bay and Haulover Bay were once important boat launching spots for

local residents, who relied heavily on their boats and boat-building skills since this was their primary means of transportation before roads were constructed. Boats were used to carry a variety of cargo including people, livestock, vegetables and fish. East Enders made regular runs to Tortola and to the market on St. Thomas. Thanks to favorable breezes, the trip to Tortola could be made on a simple "reach" and did not require time-consuming course changes. It was far easier for an East Ender to reach Tortola by boat than to get to most other places on St. John. Thus it was not at all uncommon for a young man from East End to be dating a young lady from Tortola, rather than having a girl friend in Cruz Bay.

*Hansen Bay*

The beaches and bays in and around the East End are lovely to look at and are great for swimming and snorkeling. This side of the island is very arid. Diehard beach-goers know that it is often sunny here when it is raining or cloudy else-

where on the island. You might want to give Vie's beach a try.
Vie charges a small fee for
access to this peaceful,
sandy swimming mecca.
Sand crabs on the beach
are fun to watch!

Vie can generally be
found in her snack bar
preparing local delicacies
such as conch fritters and
pates.

## Picking Up The Trail

When you have finished
exploring East End, return
to Coral Bay and pick up
the trail at the Emmaus
Moravian Church, heading
South on Route 107. The
road eventually takes you
to Salt Pond Beach and
Lameshur Beach, two
excellent beaches for
swimming and snorkeling.

Notice the mangrove
swamps along the water's
edge as you are passing
through Coral Bay.
Mangroves thrive in the
salt water and play a key
role in maintaining St.
John's ecological balance.

# Mangroves

Red mangroves populate the shoreline in many areas around St. John. Mangroves are identified by their seemingly impenetrable tangle of aerial roots seen sprouting up from the saltwater environment. The leaves of the mangrove when shed, decompose among the roots and provide nourishment for small crabs and worms, which in turn provide food for larger fish and birds. Runoff from the land dilutes the salinity of the mangrove swamps and filters out debris that might otherwise find its way to the open sea. The aerial roots also help to reduce the effects of wave damage and subsequent erosion.

## Exploring the South Side

The coastline along this section of the road offers fabulous views of the seascape. A short ways past the Shipwreck Landing, the road passes Sweet's Daily Breeze and John's Folly Beach. Watch for Mr. Sweet's handmade sign announcing his beachfront concession.

It is a great spot for exploring the reefs, and Mr. Sweet will be happy to rent you snorkel equipment. Ask him about seahorses and where to look for them!

Leaving Sweet's and continuing south on Route 107, you soon pass the entrance to the Concordia Resort. This is an eco-resort designed by Stanley Selengut, who also developed Maho Bay Campground *(See Maho Bay Camps, pg. 71).*

A short distance further you arrive at the parking area and path leading down to Salt Pond Beach.

## Salt Pond Beach

It is an easy down hill walk (0.2 miles) to Salt Pond Beach.

*Concordia Resort Seen From Salt Pond Beach*

However, the hike back up is a bit more strenuous!

Salt Pond Beach is an idyllic white, crescent-shaped stretch of sand. It has become very popular with visitors. The beach has a bounty of shells and broken pieces of coral. Snorkelers will have a wonderful time skirting the rocky shore on either side of the beach looking at the colorful fish.

# Arid Plants

Many of St. John's plants have adapted to the dry conditions that exist in certain areas of the island such as at Salt Pond Beach and Lameshur Bay. Thanks to elaborate root systems and thick, heat resistant skins that slow the process of evaporation, they thrive in these arid areas. Vegetation common to these areas includes:

## Century Plants

Tall plants that stretch as high as 20 feet or more. This plant has to grow for nearly ten years (which could seem like a century!) before it will burst forth with its yellow blooms and then die. The dead trees are used locally as the traditional Christmas tree.

## Pope's Head or Barrel Cactus

Small rounded cactus with a cardinal red head that bears a very tasty fruit.

## Dildo or Pipe Organ Cactus

Large pipe-like cactus whose size and descriptive name make it easily identifiable. Often stretching 10-25 feet tall, the Dildo or Pipe Organ cactus has a thick skin with prickly needles. The meat of the cactus is used in some local food dishes.

## Opuntia

Spreading cactus with flattened pods.

## Pinguin (wild pineapple)

Features long green leaves that look something like a pineapple. During Danish times, planters used to grow pinguin around the windows of their estate houses to keep prowlers away. Don't touch! The plant's sharp thorny surface can hurt. Pinguin produces an orange berry, which can be cooked and used as a beverage.

The vegetation around Salt Pond Beach is largely cactus and stunted, windswept growth. The beach itself takes its name from the salt pond located directly behind the trees at the far end of the beach. You will find several small paths leading from the beach to the salt pond. Salt ponds produce salt through a process of evaporation. Salt water seeps into the pond underground from the sea. As the wind blows across the surface of the pond, the water evaporates, leaving a foamy residue of sea salt. The residue eventually crystallizes and is ready for harvesting during the summer months.

At the far end (south side) of Salt Pond Beach, visitors can follow a trail, which goes out to Ram Head (a steep rocky cliff jutting out into the water). The Ram Head Trail is about 1.0 mile in length (going and returning) and takes about a half hour to walk, each way.

Escaped slaves or maroons often took refuge in this area of the island. They were able to live off the abundance of fish that could be caught near the shore. Certain varieties of cactus also supplied liquids and edible fruit. Runaway slaves also enjoyed the vantage point afforded by Ram Head, which gave them ample opportunity to hide from planters who might come looking to apprehend them.

## Moving Along

The next and last stop on the tour is Lameshur Bay. This is a lovely beach and the swimming and snorkeling are good. There are picnic tables and public restrooms. At Lameshur you can also see the remains of a bay still. Most car rental agencies ask visitors not to take their rental vehicles to Lameshur. The trip definitely requires 4-wheel drive. If you opt to take the trip on foot, leave your vehicle safely at the beginning of the dirt road, which starts about 0.5 miles past

Salt Pond Beach. The hike out to Lameshur Bay is about 1.0 mile. There is a steep hill at the beginning, but then the road flattens out and is relatively easy to walk.

## Lameshur Bay

Strolling along the beach at Lameshur, you will find shells and bits of coral tossed idly about by the surf. The warm waters and shoals off St. John make this some of the best beach-combing territory in the world. There is good snorkeling on the west side of the beach where you can readily identify many different varieties of colorful reef fish.

*Common Shells*

# Common Reef Fish

The reefs and inland waters off St. John team with a kaleidoscopic array of fish. Trying to identify a specific type of fish from the nearly 400 varieties that inhabit the area can be a daunting task for even the most experienced diver. Many fish can be recognized by their color, markings and the shape of their anatomy. But there is often such variation within a specific fish variety that other traits must sometimes be used for identification. Habitat and fish behavior will often aid identification. Many fish varieties congregate in

*Courtesy OAR/NURP*

groups called schools. They do this primarily for hunting and for self-protection from larger predators. One of the most fascinating varieties of fish is the "cleaner" fish. Cleaners are tiny fish that actually clean par-

*Portion of Illustration By John Dawson, Courtesy National Park Service*

asites and other debris from the insides of gills and mouths of larger fish. Cleaner fish like gobies literally set up "cleaning stations" at specific locations on coral reefs where they wait for larger fish like groupers that actually come looking for the cleaner fish in order to get themselves scrubbed out.

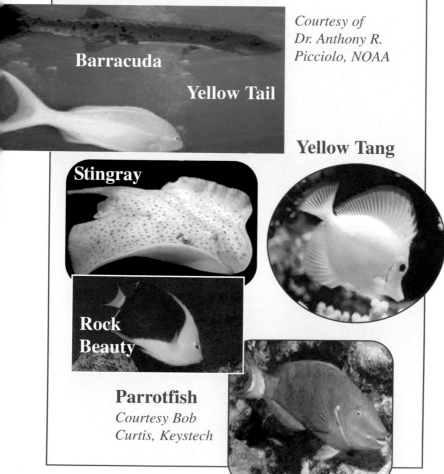

*Courtesy of Dr. Anthony R. Picciolo, NOAA*

**Barracuda**

**Yellow Tail**

**Yellow Tang**

**Stingray**

**Rock Beauty**

**Parrotfish**
*Courtesy Bob Curtis, Keystech*

# Sargeant Major

## Smooth Trunkfish

## Foureye Butterfish

*Note: Drawings of Sargeant Major, Smooth Trunkfish and Foureye Butterfish represent portions of an illustration by John Dawson, Courtesy National Park Service.*

On the hillside above the beach, you can find the remains of the Lameshur Bay rum still. The building beyond the still was probably a warehouse used to store bay oil until it could be shipped to St. Thomas. There is also a loading platform on the seaward side of the hill just below the still.

Just around the eastern point of Lameshur Bay is where

the pioneering Tektite mission took place in 1969. Three astronauts, Ed Clifton, Richard Waller and Conrad Mahnken lived in an underwater habitat for a record-breaking 58 straight days. The men conducted a variety of underwater scientific experiments and demonstrated for the first time that men could live indefinitely underwater with no apparent physiological effects. All that is left of the 18-foot tall, twin tower habitat today are the three concrete footings that supported the structure.

*This concludes the tour of Centerline and the east and south sides.*

# Reef Bay Trail Hike

A trip to St. John seems somehow incomplete without an invigorating hike down the Reef Bay Trail. The trail descends 937 feet through moist and dry forests and takes you through four sugar estates, Old Works, Hope, Josie Gut and Par Force, before arriving at the remains of the Reef Bay sugar mill near

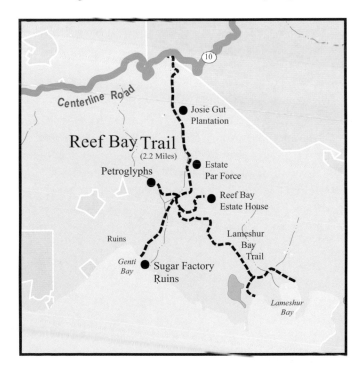

the beach at Genti Bay. This was the last operating sugar mill on St. John. The mill at Estate Reef Bay was converted to steam power in 1855. Much of the machinery is amazingly well intact.

A highlight of the hike is a visit to St. John's famous "petroglyphs" or rock carvings. They are located at a freshwater pool hidden deep in the forest. Most of the carved images are thought to be the handiwork of the Taino Indians, who lived on St. John around 1000 A.D. Some speculate that a few of the drawings may have been done by runaway slaves, while in hiding during the slave revolt of 1733.

The 2.2-mile hike from Centerline to the beach at Reef Bay is pleasant. All down hill! Along the way, you will learn about many exotic trees and plants, which are identified by informative park service markers. It is about a 2-hour hike from Centerline to the beach. To avoid the walk back up, you can make arrangements to take the hike under the supervision of a park service ranger and have the option of returning by boat to Cruz Bay. There is a charge for the return boat trip. Call the national park service in Cruz Bay for reservations.

Plan on spending the better part of a day. Pack a lunch, bring water and by all means wear comfortable shoes, not sandals. The beach at Genti Bay is excellent for swimming.

## Getting Started

As you begin to descend the trail you immediately become aware of the dense vegetation seen growing along

*Teyer Palm*

the path. This portion of the trail can get very damp and is dominated by larger trees such as the kapok, locust, monkey pistol and mango. Anthuriums, aloe, philodendrons, orchids and ferns are a few of the plants that thrive in this sub-tropical climate, as does the Teyer palm - the only palm indigenous to St. John.

Along the trail you are also likely to see many woodland creatures including lizards, hermit crabs, spiders and, of course, the ubiquitous wild donkey. Bats, rats, mongooses and many other inhabitants live here as well.

Termites have created huge brown ball-like houses seen dangling from tree trunks. Termites do not kill living trees, even though they use them to support their homes. Termites are blind insects that access dead wood on the ground and elsewhere by traveling through tunnels through which they find their way by following one another's scents.

*Termite Nest*

# St. John Plants

There are over 1000 varieties of plants growing on St. John. While some of the plants are indigenous, many came from other lands. Some were carried here on ocean currents and others were blown here by the wind. Still others were carried to St. John as unofficial passengers on merchant ships or by slaves brought here from Africa. Plants played an important role in the daily lives of early

St. Johnians who were used to "making do." Plants supplied food for animals and people. They were used as building materials and many were fashioned into household implements. Fisherman used plants to craft fish traps and nets and some plants were used in local industries like basket making.

Plants were also used in folk (or "bush") medicines to treat a variety of ailments. For example, aloe, which is commonly found along the Reef Bay Trail, was used in the treatment of colds, asthma, ulcers, burns and insect bites. The leaf of the plant can be slit in two and the jelly extracted and applied to the face to remove wrinkles.

The following is a partial checklist of some of the more common plants found at places like the Reef Bay Trail, Cinnamon Bay, Annaberg, Salt Pond and Lameshur.

### Anthurium *(Anthurium cordatum)*

There are over 500 varieties of these plants, which are native to Central and South America and the Caribbean Islands. Anthuriums are perennials that grow on the ground or up in trees. Heart leaf anthuriums produce beautiful foliage. The pistil of the plant forms a long green "whip."

## Calabash *(Crescentia cujeta)*

The leaf is used in tea to treat colds, diarrhea, dysentery and headaches. The fruit, when roasted, is said to be good for treatment of menstrual cramps and to induce childbirth. The gourd-like fruit was often scooped out and used for bowls, musical instruments and drinking cups. The raw pulp of the fruit is said to be poisonous and has proven toxic to birds.

## Kapok

*(Eriodendron anfractuosum)*
The kapok is found along the upper portions of the Reef Bay Trail as well as at Cinnamon Bay and Cancel Bay. Kapok or silk cotton trees are used in manufacturing

life preservers and were used locally to make pillows.

## Locust *(Hymenea courbail)*

The durable wood of this handsome tree is used for furniture, shipbuilding and fence posts. The tree produces large dark red pods containing several seeds surrounded by a strong-smelling yellow pulp, which gives this tree the local name of "stinkin' toe tree." The pulp is edible and sweet tasting. There are some large locust trees along the trail. The base of the tree is similar to the kapok, but the trunk of the locust is straighter and more stately in appearance.

## Maran *(Croton discolor)*

Found in arid areas such as Salt Pond Beach at East End and on the lower portion of the Reef Bay Trail. Prepared as a medicinal tea, the leaves are thought to be an effective folk remedy for bladder trouble, gonorrhea and rheumatism. Rough fuzzy-like leaves are handy for scrubbing pots and pans.

## Tamarind
*(Tamarindus indicus)*
Tamarinds are used in making preserves and the seed filled pods can be used to make a very tasty drink.

## Wild Tamarind *(Leucaena glauca)*
Grows prolifically throughout the Virgin Islands.

## Turpentine *(Bursera simaruba)*
This spreading aromatic native of the West Indies is recognized by its smooth reddish bark, which peels off in papery flakes. A turpentine like smell is given off by the tree resin. This resin has been used in glue, varnish and incense. Other

common names for the tree include gumbo, limbo, tourist nose and lying fence post tree. This last name suggests the once common use of this tree on St. John.

### Wandering Jew *(Zebrina pendula)*

Introduced from Mexico, this shade loving plant has pointed oval leaves with purple, green and silvery stripes. Its leaves have been used as a tea to treat high blood pressure. Found in many areas including along the Reef Bay Trail.

The first readily visible ruins that you come to along the trail are those of the Jose Gut Sugar Estate, located about a half-mile from Centerline Road. After passing the remains of a former corral, you come to a circular platform. This is where the horsemill that powered the cane crushers was once located.

About a half-mile further on, you arrive at the skeletal remains of a small house at Estate Par Force. The house was built in the 1930s and owned by Miss Anna Marsh, a native St. Johnian who was murdered here at Reef Bay in 1938. Miss Marsh was a descendant of Mr. William Henry Marsh, who arrived on St. John from England around 1850. Mr. Marsh managed the Reef Bay sugar plantation before purchasing it at auction in 1864. He married a St. Johnian woman and had ten children. Anna Marsh was one of his four daughters. At the time of her death, she owned quite a bit of property in the area, including the Reef Bay sugar mill and estate house. Miss Marsh's assailant was apprehended when he tried to sell her gold ring on St. Thomas.

## Estate Par Force

Like most of the early plantations on St. John, we do not know a great deal about the history of Par Force. It was in existence as early as 1780. One of the estate's first recorded owners was Anthony Zytzema. Following Zytzema's death, the property changed hands a number of times until finally being purchased by John Vetters, a man of substantial wealth, sometime around 1830. About the same time, Vetters also acquired the Reef Bay Estate, which was at the time a small tract of land skirting the beach below. The two estates, Par Force and Reef Bay, then became one large estate called the Reef Bay Plantation. Vetters had a new sugar factory constructed on the beach at Reef Bay, which replaced operations at the Old Par Force factory.

In 1855, the plantation was sold to O.J. Bergeest and Company. It was during Bergeest's ownership that steam power was installed at the Reef Bay factory. After acquiring the property in 1864, William Marsh was able to profitably run the plantation for the next 50 years despite increasing labor costs and declining interest in West Indian cane. Marsh died in 1909 and two of his four daughters continued to run the operation and managed to keep producing sugar until 1916, when the sugar mill was finally shut down for good.

In 1955, the property was purchased by the Jackson Hole Preserve and subsequently donated to the federal government along with other holdings for the purpose of creating the Virgin Islands National Park.

About a mile beyond Par Force, you will come to a trail marker leading to the petroglyphs. In recent years, St. John's famous rock carvings have become the subject of new speculation.

## Petroglyphs

Most of these mysterious carvings with their strange and seemingly primitive designs are now believed to be the work of the Taino Indians. The waterfall (which is usually flowing) is thought to be a sacred meeting place where religious rites were once practiced. Fresh-water crayfish and algae can be found in the pool at the foot of the waterfall. It is interesting to speculate as to how fresh water animals could have found their way here.

After retracing your steps to the main trail you come to a sign pointing off to the left toward Lameshur Bay. This is also the way to reach the Reef Bay Estate House. The path to the estate house is sometimes overgrown and difficult to follow. However, if you are dressed properly and have the extra energy, you should be able to find your way safely up the steep hillside to the estate house at the top. To reach the estate house, you start out by following the Lameshur Bay Trail.

When the path forks (about 0.1 mile ahead) you go left. Keep heading up the hill, and you will eventually get there.

## Reef Bay Estate House

The Reef Bay Estate House was built in 1832 and renovated in 1844. In 1994, the park service began restoring the house, but the work was never completed. Like most great houses on St. John, the Reef Bay Estate House was built on a hilltop to take advantage of the cool ocean breezes.

The main building has been closed to prevent vandalism, but feel free to wander about the grounds (provided the bush has been cut back by the park service). At the rear of the building you will find the remains of a stable and outhouse. The structure to the right of the gate is a cookhouse.

Leaving the estate house, find your way back down the path to the main trail leading to Reef Bay.

## Valley Floor

The path from here to the beach is flat. The climate on the valley floor is considerably drier than along the upper portions of the trail. Early residents planted several different varieties of citrus trees along the path leading through the valley floor. If you look carefully, you can still spot lime trees growing close to the edge of the trail. Just before reaching the beach, you will come to a marshy area where you will see many holes in the ground. The holes are made by land crabs. They were once highly sought after by locals as a delicacy. Because of their dwindling numbers, catching land crabs is now strictly prohibited by the park service.

## Reef Bay Sugar Factory

The Reef Bay factory was constructed around 1830 and

enlarged and modernized to accommodate steam power in 1860. It is one of the best examples of a sugar factory still standing on St. John. Its huge flywheel, heavy rollers, and much of its steam-powered equipment are surprisingly well preserved. Working around the machinery, when it was operating, could be very dangerous. You had to be very careful. In 1908, a fifteen-year-old boy got caught in the cogs and was crushed to death.

Once cane was cut and processed in the factory building, it was next shipped to Europe from Reef Bay Estate aboard sailing vessels that would anchor in the bay. Dories were employed to transport the sugar to the waiting ships. The boats were tipped on their side to permit the heavy barrels or "hogsheads" of sugar to be rolled inside. They were then righted, and the sugar was carried to the waiting ships where

it was lifted aboard and stored in cargo holds for the long journey.

The Reef Bay sugar mill appears to be in remarkably good condition. Letting the imagination wander, one can almost see the giant flywheel start to turn and hear the hissing of steam from the large boiler as the sweet aroma of fresh cane juice suddenly floods the air.

*This concludes the hike down The Reef Bay Trail.*

## Facts and Figures

The Virgin Islands of the United States is a U.S. territory. It is located in the Lesser Antilles at 18 degrees North latitude and 65 degrees West longitude. The 1990 population of the Virgin Islands was 98,000. The capital is Charlotte Amalie on St. Thomas. The Department of the Interior administers the Virgin Islands. They have a locally elected governor and senate. Residents do not get to vote in Presidential elections, but they do send an elected representative to Congress. Virgin Islanders pay federal income taxes, but the collected revenues are retained in the local treasury. The U.S. dollar is the official currency. The Virgin Islands operate on Atlantic Standard Time, which is one hour ahead of Eastern Standard Time or the same as Day Light Savings Time. When traveling to the Virgin Islands, U.S. citizens do not need passports, but some form of ID is required. A birth certificate or photo driver's license will do. Foreigners require appropriate international documentation.

## Power and Telephone Communications

In the Virgin Islands, standard 110 volts/60 Hz electrical power is used, so there is no need for stateside visitors to bring adapters for hair dryers, computers and other electrical necessities. Power outages do occur, but they do not last long. Cell phone service is available in the U.S. Virgin Islands. Some cell phones supplied by stateside service providers also work in the U.S. Virgin Islands. Others do not. If you find that your cell phone provider does not service the U.S. Virgin Islands, you can still use your cell phone when you get here by purchasing temporary service through one of the local providers.

## How to Get Here!

Unless you are coming by boat, you must first fly to St. Thomas in order to reach St. John. Major airlines fly directly to St. Thomas from New York, Boston and Miami. There are excellent connecting flights through Puerto Rico. From the St. Thomas airport you take a 45-minute taxi ride to Red Hook on the eastern end of St. Thomas, where you catch the ferry to Cruz Bay, St. John. The Red Hook ferry costs $3.00

each way and runs on the hour from 6:00 a.m. - 11:00 p.m. The ferry ride between Red Hook and Cruz Bay takes 20 minutes. Less frequent ferries run between downtown Charlotte Amalie and Cruz Bay (45-minute ride). For more information call Transportation Services (340-776-6282).

## Climate and Clothing

Temperatures range from the low-70s to the mid-90s year round. Hurricane season runs from June through October. The cooler months are December through April. The rainfall is usually more frequent from July to January. It can get quite dry in the spring and summer. Passing showers are common at any time of the year.

As far as clothing is concerned, cottons are best. A light jacket or sweater may be needed during the evenings of the cooler months.

# Banking

The bank in Cruz Bay village is equipped with an ATM that accepts NYCE, CIRRUS and PLUS with PIN#. It also takes MC and VISA.

# Water Conservation

Conserving water is a way of life on St. John. Islanders rely on infrequent rain showers to collect fresh water in their cisterns. Most hotels, guest homes and villas ask visitors to be frugal with their use of this precious commodity.

# Hurricanes

These storms have occasionally caused severe damage in the Virgin Islands. Watch weather forecasts and plan accordingly. Most hotels will not allow guests to stay during a hurricane. If you are unable to make a timely exit from the island, you will be required to take shelter at a designated location.

# Local Holidays

*THREE KINGS DAY* (**January 6**)

*TRANSFER DAY* (**March 31**)
   Commemorates the sale of the Virgin Islands to the U.S.

*ST. JOHN FESTIVAL* (**June-July**)
   Thirty-day event encompassing Organic Act Day (third Monday in June), Carnival (1st week of July) and Emancipation Day (July 3rd).

*HURRICANE SUPPLICATION DAY* (**4th Monday in July**)

*LOCAL THANKSGIVING* (3rd **Monday in October**)

## Accommodations, Restaurants, Shopping, Water Sports, Beaches, Real Estate, etc…..

St. John offers a wide variety of accommodations and restaurants to suit everyone's budget and taste. Water Sports, shopping and beaches are all in abundance. Visitors will find the following internet sites helpful when looking for accommodations and planning activities:

http://www.stjohnusvi.com

http://www.usvi.net/usvi/stj.html

*Weston Resort*

## Campgrounds and Eco-Resorts

(1) Cinnamon Bay Campground
P.O. Box 720
St. John, USVI 00831
(340) 776-6330     (340) 776-6458 (fax)

(2)  Maho Bay Camps, Inc.
17A East 73rd Street, New York, NY 10021
(212) 472-9453  E-mail:    mahony org @maho

*Concordia Resort*
*c/o Maho Bay Camps*

# Virgin Islands National Park

The park service has made available some very useful information for the visiting public. You may contact the park service by writing or calling them at:

Virgin Islands National Park
P.O. Box 710
St. John, USV.I. 00831
(340) 776-6201

Learn more about park service activities and resources by visiting their website at:
http://www.nps.gov/viis

# Publications about St. John:

These books are on sale at the National Park Visitor Information Center in Cruz Bay and in several of the gift shops in town.

**Anderson, John L.** 1975. Night of the Silent Drums, A Narrative of Slave Rebellion in the Virgin Islands. New York: Charles Scribner's Sons.

**Benjamin, Guy.** 1998. Me and My Beloved Virgin. USA.

**Bond, James.** 1993. A Field Guide to Birds of the West Indies. Boston: Houghton Mifflin Company.

**Hull, Ruth Low and Valls, Rafael**. 1985. St. John Backtime, Eyewitness Accounts from 1718 to 1956. St. John, United States Virgin Islands: Eden Hill Press.

**Humann, Paul**. 1989. Reef Fish Identification. Jacksonville, Florida: New World Publications, Inc.

**Humann, Paul**. 1989. Reef Coral Identification. Jacksonville, Florida: New World Publications, Inc.

**Jadan, Doris**. 1985. A Guide to the Natural History of St. John. St. Thomas, V.I.: Environmental Studies Program, Inc.

**Nellis, David W**. 1997. Poisonous Plants and Animals of Florida and the Caribbean. Sarasota, Florida: Pineapple Press, Inc.

**Rouse, Irving**. 1992. The Tainos, Rise & Decline of the People Who Greeted Columbus. New Haven & London: Yale University Press.

**Singer, Gerald**. 1994. The St. John Beach Guide. St. John, USVI: Sombrero Publishing Co.

**Singer, Gerald**. 1996. St. John Off the Beaten Track. St. John, USVI: Sombrero Publishing Co.

*"No matter how fast*
*moonlight run,*
*daylight catches up."*
- Local Proverb